THE LANGUAGE GYM

SPANISH SENTENCE BUILDERS

A lexicogrammar approach

Beginner to Pre-Intermediate

LISTENING

Student Book

Exercises and activities

 **THE LANGUAGE GYM**

Imprint: Independently Published

Edited by Verónica Palacín

DEDICATION

For Catrina

- Gianfranco

For Ariella and Leonard

- Dylan

ABOUT THE AUTHORS

Gianfranco Conti taught for 25 years at schools in Italy, the UK and in Kuala Lumpur, Malaysia. He has also been a university lecturer, holds a Master's degree in Applied Linguistics and a PhD in metacognitive strategies as applied to second language writing. He is now an author, a popular independent educational consultant and professional development provider. He has written around 2,000 resources for the TES website, which have awarded him the Best Resources Contributor in 2015. He has co-authored the best-selling and influential book for world languages teachers, "The Language Teacher Toolkit" and "Breaking the Sound Barrier: Teaching Learners how to Listen", in which he puts forth his Listening As Modelling methodology. Gianfranco writes an influential blog on second language acquisition called The Language Gym, co-founded the interactive website language-gym.com and the Facebook professional group Global Innovative Language Teachers (GILT). Last but not least, Gianfranco has created the instructional approach known as E.P.I. (Extensive Processing Instruction).

Dylan Viñales has taught for 15 years, in schools in Bath, Beijing and Kuala Lumpur in state, independent and international settings. He lives in Kuala Lumpur. He is fluent in five languages, and gets by in several more. Dylan is, besides a teacher, a professional development provider, specialising in E.P.I., metacognition, teaching languages through music (especially ukulele) and cognitive science. In the last five years, together with Dr Conti, he has driven the implementation of E.P.I. in one of the top international schools in the world: Garden International School. This has allowed him to test, on a daily basis, the sequences and activities included in this book with excellent results (his students have won language competitions both locally and internationally). He has designed an original Spanish curriculum, bespoke instructional materials, based on Reading and Listening as Modelling (RAM and LAM). Dylan co-founded the fastest growing professional development group for modern languages teachers on Facebook, Global Innovative Languages Teachers, which includes over 12,000 teachers from all corners of the globe. He authors an influential blog on modern language pedagogy in which he supports the teaching of languages through E.P.I. Dylan is the lead author of Spanish content on the Language Gym website and oversees the technological development of the site. He is currently undertaking the NPQML qualification, after which he plans to pursue a Masters in second language acquisition.

ACKNOWLEDGEMENTS

Many thanks to the native speakers who contributed to the recording process. In particular, thanks to José Luis Larrosa, Andrea Lobo, Roberto Jover Soro, Alejandra López Tejedor, Inés Glowacka, Carlota Viguer Serina and Verónica Palacín for their time and effort in recording the sound files.

Secondly, our thanks and appreciation to the testing and proofreading team, Alfonso Maldonado, Ronan Jezequel, Julien Barrett, Tom Ball, Tom Weidner, Simona Gravina, Stefano Pianigiani, Miquél Marti Danés and Roberto Jover Soro. It is thanks to their time, patience and professionalism that we have been able to produce such a refined and highly accurate product.

EXTENSIVE PROCESSING INSTRUCTION

If you have bought into our E.P.I. approach

Both this listening book and the original Sentence Builder book were originally designed as a resource to use in conjunction with our E.P.I. approach and teaching strategies. Our course favours flooding comprehensible input, organising content by communicative functions and related constructions, and a big focus on reading and listening as modelling. The aim of these books is to empower the beginner-to-pre-intermediate learner with linguistic tools - high-frequency structures and vocabulary - useful for real-life communication.

If you don't know or have NOT yet bought into our approach

If you would like to learn about E.P.I. you could read one of the authors' blogs. The definitive guide is Dr Conti's "Patterns First – How I Teach Lexicogrammar" which can be found on his blog (www.gianfrancoconti.com). There are also informative and user-friendly blogs on Dylan's Wordpress site (mrvinalesmfl.wordpress.com) such as "Using sentence builders to reduce (everyone's) workload and create more fluent linguists" which can be read to get teaching ideas and to learn how to structure a course, through all the stages of E.P.I.

The book "Breaking the Sound Barrier: Teaching Learners how to Listen" by Gianfranco Conti and Steve Smith, provides a detailed description of the approach and of the listening and speaking activities you can use in synergy with the present book.

INTRODUCTION

This Spanish Listening Booklet matches to the minutest details the content of the 19 units included in the best-selling workbook for beginner-to-pre-intermediate learners "Spanish sentence builders", by the same authors. For best results, the two books should be used together.

This book fully implements Dr Conti's popular approach to listening-skills instruction, L.A.M. (aka *Listening-As-Modelling*), laid out in his seminal work: "Breaking the Sound Barrier: Teaching Learners how to Listen" (Conti and Smith, 2019). L.A.M. is based on the concept that listening instruction should train students in the mastery of the key micro-listening skills identified by cognitive psychologists as follows:

- Phonemic processing
- Syllable processing
- Segmenting
- Lexical retrieval
- Parsing
- Meaning building
- Discourse building

This translates into aural instruction which deliberately targets the above micro-abilities through a range of tasks performed on input which is (1) highly patterned; (2) 90-98 % comprehensible; (3) flooded with the occurrence of the target structural patterns and lexical items; (4) delivered at a rate of speed which allows for learning; (5) designed to induce a priming effect on learning (i.e. to subconsciously sensitize the learners to the target language items).

Each unit contains around 13 listening tasks, which provide continuous and extensive recycling of the target constructions and vocabulary items and address the development of the key listening micro-skills. The tasks include engaging and tested Conti classics such as "Spot the intruder", "Missing details", "Faulty transcript", "Break the flow", "Faulty translation", "Gapped translation" and "Listening slalom", alongside more traditional listening comprehension tasks.

The tasks have been designed with the following key L.A.M. principles in mind: (1) the task's cognitive load must be appropriate to the level of the target learners; (2) the tasks must involve thorough processing (i.e. they should promote attention to details); (3) at the beginning stages, the tasks should promote noticing of the target language items by creating opportunities for cognitive comparison between the target language and the mother tongue (e.g. by using parallel texts in both languages, as happens in tasks such as "Bad translation" and "Gapped translation"); (4) the tasks should provide the learners with multiple entry points for acquisition by requiring them to engage with the same or similar texts at different levels of processing (from the identification of sounds to lexical retrieval; from the processing of structural patterns to the construction of meaning and discourse); (5) the tasks should model speaking micro-skills (e.g. pronunciation, decoding skills, functional and positional processing), not merely exam-taking techniques (as textbooks typically do); (6) tasks should be sequenced in a graded fashion, gradually phasing out support and increasing in difficulty.

The tasks have been tested countless times with students aged 11 to 13, with very positive feedback both in terms of engagement and perceived effectiveness. In particular, Dylan has been a pioneer of the approach and used it exclusively, and extensively, over the last 4 years at Garden International School, with excellent results in terms of both student engagement and progress.

HOW TO USE THIS BOOK

This book was intended as a Listening-for-learning tool aimed at paving the way for spoken and/or written production. If used in conjunction with the "Spanish Sentence Builders" book, the tasks in each unit would follow the presentational stage of the target constructions through sentence builders and associated teacher-led aural activities aimed at building phonological awareness (e.g. "Faulty echo", "Minimal pairs", "Spot the silent letters", "Write it as you hear it") and at establishing meaning (e.g. "Listening bingo", "Positive or Negative", "Faulty transcript").

We recommend interspersing the listening tasks in each unit with engaging vocabulary-building, reading and read-aloud activities rather than covering every single exercise in a sequential fashion. Also, teachers, in selecting the activities and crafting each instructional sequence, should be cognizant of the motivational levels and concentration span of their students. These will vary from class to class and will inevitably inform their choice of the amount and type of listening that will be most conducive to learning.

Please note that whilst the sequence in which the tasks are arranged in each unit was carefully crafted by the authors to provide a graded and balanced progression from easier to more challenging, teachers should not feel straight-jacketed by that order.

If the teacher has near native or native command of the target language, they may want to deliver some of activities by reading the text aloud themselves using the transcripts provided in the accompanying teacher book (bought separately). This will enable them to enhance the input by emphasizing specific aspects of the input (e.g. specific words, word endings or phonotactic features such as assimilation phenomena) they may want their students to notice. Input enhancement is a useful means to enhance acquisition and interpersonal listening whereby the teacher interacts with the learners is an effective way to make aural input more learnable, engaging and motivational.

ACCESSING THE SOUND FILES

The sound files can be accessed at www.language-gym.com/listening (password is "**penguin**").

Once you log on, you will see a menu, containing all the units in the book, ordered and labelled as per the book itself.

IMPORTANT NOTICE: Please note, that this section of the Language Gym can be accessed by any person who has bought this book, regardless of whether or not you are a subscriber to the main Language Gym site. Under no circumstances should this password be shared with a teacher, **outside of your school**, who has not bought the book. This extends to other schools inside a collective of schools, such as a trust. In brief: every school should buy their own book. The book should not be shared outside of your school.

CHOOSING A DIFFICULTY LEVEL

Please note that several activities contain a normal and a "harder" or "faster" version. These have been added in as a differentiation tool. It is up to the individual teacher's discretion which file to use, based on their knowledge of the students in their classes.

TABLE OF CONTENTS

Unit	Title	Communicative function	Page
1	Talking about my age	Describing yourself and other people	1
	Decoding Skills – Part 1		3
2	Saying when my birthday is	Describing yourself and other people	4
	Decoding Skills – Part 2		7
3	Describing hair and eyes	Describing yourself and other people	8
	Decoding Skills – Part 3		11
4	Saying where I live and am from	Indicating location	12
	Decoding Skills – Part 4		15
5	Talking about my family members (age and relationships)	Describing people and relationships	16
	Decoding Skills – Part 5		19
6	Describing myself and another family member	Describing people, relationships and expressing opinions	20
7	Talking about pets	Describing people/animals and asking questions	23
8	Talking about jobs	Describing people, expressing opinions and indicating location	26
9	Comparing people's appearance and personality	Comparing and contrasting	29
10	Saying what's in my school bag / classroom	Stating what you have and describing objects	32
	Reading Aloud – Part 1		35
11	Talking about food - Introduction	Describing food and expressing opinions	36
12	Talking about food - Likes / dislikes	Describing routine behaviour in the present, expressing opinions	39
13	Talking about clothes and accessories	Describing people, routine behaviour in the present and indicating time	42
14	Saying what I and others do in our free time	Describing routine behaviour in the present and indicating time	45
	Reading Aloud – Part 2		48
15	Talking about weather and free time	Describing events and routine behaviour in the present and indicating location	49
16	Talking about my daily routine	Describing routine behaviour in the present, indicating time, sequencing	52
17	Describing my house	Indicating location, describing things and expressing likes/dislikes	55
18	Saying what I do at home / daily routine	Indicating routine behaviour in the present, time, frequency and location	58
	Reading Aloud – Part 3		61
19	Talking about future plans and holidays	Making plans for the future, indicating time, location and expressing opinions	62

UNIT 1 – TALKING ABOUT MY AGE

1. Fill in the blanks

a. Me __ __ __ __ __ Alejandro.

b. Tengo __ __ __ __ __ __ años.

c. Tengo __ __ __ hermanos.

d. __ __ hermano mayor se __ __ __ __ __ Roberto.

e. Mi __ __ __ __ __ __ __ __ menor __ __ llama Julián.

f. ¿Cómo __ __ llamas tú?

g. ¿Cuántos __ __ __ __ tienes?

2. Break the flow (draw a line between each word)

a. MellamoAntonioytengodoceaños

b. Tengoquinceaños

c. MihermanosellamaPedro

d. MihermanasellamaArantxa

e. ¿Cuántosañostienes?

f. MihermanosellamaFelipe

g. ¿Cómotellamas?

3. Arrange in the correct order

I am thirteen years old	
Arantxa is fifteen years old	
My name is Paco	**1**
My sister is called Arantxa	
I have a brother and a sister	
My brother is called Fernando	
Fernando is thirteen years old	

4. Spot the differences and correct your text

a. Me llamo Karina.

b. Tengo once años.

c. Tengo dos hermanas.

d. Mi hermano mayor se llama Pepe.

e. Mi hermano mayor se llama Roberto.

f. Paco tiene catorce años.

g. Roberto tiene ocho años.

h. ¿Cuántos años tengo?

5. Faulty translation: spot the translation errors and correct them

a. Her name is Andrea.

b. I am from Argentina.

c. I have three brothers.

d. My older sister is called Amparo.

e. My younger sister is called Luana.

f. Amparo is ten.

g. Luana is fourteen.

h. I am eleven.

6. Spot the missing words and write them in

a. ______ me llamo Pedro.

b. Soy España.

c. Tengo trece ______ .

d. Tengo un hermano ______ una hermana.

e. Mi hermano ______ llama Roberto.

f. ______ hermana se llama Isabel.

g. Roberto ______ catorce años.

7. Listen, spot and correct the errors

a. Tengo catorce año

b. Me llama Carlos

c. Mi hermano se llamo Pablo

d. Tengo dos hermano

e. Tengo uno hermano y una hermana

f. ¿Cuánto años tienes?

8. Listen and fill in the grid

	Age	Brothers	Sisters
María			
José			
Paco			
Arantxa			
Emilia			
Amparo			

9. Complete with the missing letters

a. Me llam__ Pedro

b. Soy d__ España

c. Tengo quin__e años

d. No tengo hermano__

e. …pero tengo un__ hermana

f. Mi hermana se llam__ Arantxa

g. Arantxa tien__ doce a__os

h. Y tú ¿Cómo t__ llamas?

i. ¿Cuántos años tiene__?

10. Translate the sentences you hear into English

1.

2.

3.

4.

5.

6.

7.

8.

9.

11. Narrow listening - Gap-fill

Me llamo ______________ . Soy de Barcelona, en ______________ . En mi familia hay cuatro personas: ______________ madre, mi padre y mis ______________ hermanos. Mi hermano ______________ se llama Miguel y mi hermano ______________ se llama Paco. Miguel tiene ______________ años y mi hermano Paco tiene ______________ años. Y tú, ¿cómo te ______________? ¿______________ años tienes?

llamas	Antonio	menor	mi	seis
mayor	quince	España	cuántos	dos

12. Narrow listening - Gapped translation

My name is ___________. I am from ___________ in Spain. In my family there are ___________ people: my mother, my father, my ___________ brother, my ___________ brother and myself. My ___________brother is called ___________.
He is ___________ years old. My ___________ brother is called Antonio. He is ___________ years old.

How about you, what ___________________________?
How ___________________________?
how___________________________?

1. Listen and Complete

a. Me llamo Ale__andra.

b. Mi __ermana se llama Isabel.

c. Mi madre se _ _ama María.

d. Mi hermano se llama Jos__.

e. Yo tengo __inco años.

f. Bel__n tiene dieciséis a__os.

g. Mi hermano menor tiene quin__e años.

h. __ulián tiene nueve años.

i. Na_ _o tiene die__ años.

2. Choose the correct spelling

	a	b
1	hermano	ermano
2	diex	diez
3	nuebe	nueve
4	siete	sete
5	once	onze
6	Aranca	Arantxa
7	Julián	Hulián
8	ocio	ocho
9	cuatro	quatro
10	quince	kince

3. Write it as you hear it – write in brackets how the letter(s) underlined sound to your ear.

a. Cinco [e.g. THINKO]

b. Quince

c. Hermano

d. Ocho

e. José

f. Año

g. Julián

h. Guillermo

i. Me llamo

4. Compare the pronunciation of the underlined letters in each pair of words. What are the similarities/differences between the two languages?

a. Cinco	a. Think
b. Quince	b. Queen
c. Hermano	c. Herman
d. Ocho	d. Beach
e. José	e. Passé
f. Año	f. Canyon
g. Julián	g. Julian
h. Guillermo	h. Guide
i. Me llamo	i. Callum
j. Geraldo	j. Gerrald

5. Spot the pronunciation mistakes

a. Año

b. Cinco

c. Hermana

d. Guillermo

e. Julián

f. Geraldo

g. José

h. Me llamo

i. Alejandro

j. Se llama

k. Generoso

l. Catorce

UNIT 2 – SAYING WHEN MY BIRTHDAY IS

1. Fill in the blanks

a. Me __ __ __ __ __ Alejandro y mi cumpleaños es __
__ quince de __ __ __ __.

b. __ __ __ llamo Pedro y __ __ cumpleaños es el __ __ __
de __ __ __ __ __.

c. Me llamo __ __ __ __ __ __ y mi cumpleaños es el __ __
__ __ de __ __ __ __ __.

d. __ __ llamo Alfonso y mi __ __ __ __ __ __ __ __ __ __
__ es el __ __ __ __ de __ __ __ __ __ __ __ __ __ __ __.

e. __ __ __ __ __ __ __ __ Pablo y mi cumpleaños __ __ el
__ __ __ __ __ __ de __ __ __ __ __ __ __ __ __ __.

2. Break the flow (draw lines between each word)

a. Micumpleañoseseltrecedeoctubre

b. Micumpleañoselnuevedemayo

c. ¿Cuándoestucumpleaños?

d. Micumpleañoseselunodeagosto

e. Micumpleañoseseldieciséisdemayo

f. ¿Cuándoessucumpleaños?

g. Mihermanotienecatorceaños

h. Sucumpleañoseseldosdeenero

3. Arrange in the correct order

Hola, me llamo Fernando	1
Tengo un hermano	
Soy mexicano	
Su cumpleaños es el cinco de marzo	
…pero vivo en Estados Unidos	
Mi cumpleaños es el trece de julio	
Tengo diez años	

4. Listen, spot and correct the errors

a. Me llamo Julián.

b. No tengo hermanos.

c. Soy hija única.

d. Soy de Perú.

e. …pero vivo en Italia.

f. Tengo quince años.

g. Mi cumpleaños es el catorce de junio.

h. Mi novia Luisa tiene trece años.

i. Su cumpleaños es el dieciocho de octubre.

5. Faulty translation: spot the translation errors and correct them

a. My name is Roberto and I am eleven years old. My birthday is on 4th July.

b. My mother's name is Arantxa. She is 28 years old. Her birthday on 13th August.

c. My father's name is Pablo. He is 39 years old. His birthday is on 10th January.

d. I have three brothers.

e. My brother Alex is 12 and his birthday is on 2nd July.

f. My brother Nico is 9 and his birthday is on 22nd May.

g. Do you have any brothers?

6. Spot and fill in the missing words

Me llamo Roberto, soy español vivo en

Argentina. Tengo doce. En mi familia hay cinco:

mi padre, mi madre, dos hermanos y yo. Mi

hermano mayor llama Pedro y hermano menor

se llama Renato. Pedro tiene quince años y

cumpleaños es doce de abril. Renato tiene nueve

años y su cumpleaños es veinte de julio.

7. Listen, spot and correct the errors

a. Mi cumpleaños el veinte de junio.

b. Mi amiga se llama Patricia. Es diez años y su cumpleaños es el quince de mayo.

c. El cumpleaños de mi amiga es en el nueve de abril.

d. Mi madre tengo treinta y ocho años y su cumpleano es el treinta de noviembre.

e. Mi amigo se llamo Roberto. Su cumpleaños es el catorce de octobre.

8. Listen and fill in the grid

	Country	Age	Birthday
Andrea			
Paco			
Nina			
Dylan			
Miguel			
Marta			

9. Complete with the missing letters

a. Me llamo Ser__io.

b. No tengo __ermanos.

c. Soy hi__o único.

d. So__ de Perú.

e. …pero viv__ en Italia.

f. Tengo quin__e años.

g. Mi cumpleaños es el catorce de __unio.

h. Mi no__ia, Carmen, tiene trece años.

i. Su cumpleaños es el diecioc__o de octubre.

10. Translate the ten sentences you hear into English

1.

2.

3.

4.

5.

6.

7.

8.

9.

10.

11. Narrow listening: gap-fill

Hola, me llamo Silvia y ______________ de Bilbao, España. Tengo ____________ años. Mi cumpleaños es el __________ de mayo. Tengo dos hermanos, Felipe y Gonzalo. Felipe __________ catorce años y su cumpleaños es el veintiuno ________ marzo. Mi hermano Gonzalo tiene dieciséis años y ____________ cumpleaños es el __________ de junio. En ___________ tenemos un hámster también. Se __________ Guapo y tiene dos años. Mi mejor ____________ se llama Magda. Tiene ____________ años. Su cumpleaños es el ____________ de enero.

12. Narrow listening: fill in the grid in English

Name	
Town	
Age	
Birthday	
Brother's age	
Brother's birthday	

13. Narrow listening - Gapped translation

____ ________ is Ariela. I am __________ years old. I am from ____________, in ___________. My birthday is on 16th ________. I have a _________ called __________. He is ________ years old. ________ birthday is on ________ December. My best friend is called ________. She is ________ years old and her birthday is on ________ ________. My ________ is called Andrea. She is ________ years old and her birthday is on ________ ________. At home we have a pet. It is a ________. ______________ Maite and it is ________ years old.

14. Listening slalom: follow the speaker from top to bottom and number the boxes accordingly

1 - Vero	2 - Leo	3 - Alejandro	4 - Gabriela	5 - Carlos
My name is Vero (1)	My brother is called Leo	My name is Alejandro	My name is Gabriela	My name is Carlos
I am from Valencia	**I am from Barbastro (1)**	I am from Barcelona	He is from Santiago	I am from Granada
He is 14	I am 21	**I am 13 (1)**	I am 9	I am 16
My birthday is on 15th March	**My birthday is on 16th July (1)**	My birthday is on 21st May	My birthday is on 23rd June	My birthday is on 30th August
I have a friend	I have a hamster	I have a boyfriend	He has a girlfriend	**I have a sister (1)**
His birthday is on 12th	Her birthday is on 7th	**Her birthday is on 1st (1)**	His birthday is on 2nd	Her birthday is on 30th
January (1)	March	October	June	September

15. Faulty translation: spot the translation errors and correct them

My name is Marco, I am from Spain. I am 13 years old. My parents are called Adolfo and Marina. They are 38 years old. My mother's birthday is on 21st March. My father's birthday is on 4th August. I have two sisters, Rafa and Antonio. Rafa is 10 years old and Antonio is 12. Rafa's birthday is on 11th July. Antonio's birthday in on 31st April. At home we have a pet, a snake. Its name is Pablo and it is one year old. I have a girlfriend. Her name is Petra. She is 14. Her birthday is on 16th September.

DECODING SKILLS UNIT 2

1. Listen and complete

a. __inco

b. o__ __o

c. die__

d. on__e

e. diecis__is

f. me __ __amo

g. mar__o

h. m__ __o

i. nov__embre

j. dic__embre

k. cumplea__os

l. cator__e

m. diecioc__o

n. ___unio

2. Write it as you hear it – listen to the alphabet and write it as you hear it

A -

B -

C -

D -

E -

F -

G -

H -

I -

J -

K -

L -

M -

N -

Ñ -

O -

P -

Q -

R -

S -

T -

U -

V -

W -

X -

Y -

Z -

Author's note: a double l is pronounced as a /y/ (like in me "llamo"). The letter "ll" however, no longer exists☹ The RAE took it out of the Spanish alphabet in 2014. There also used to be a "ch", which was also lost.

3. Tick the letter you hear

	a	b	c
1	J	H	G
2	L	LL	N
3	X	Y	J
4	E	I	Y
5	C	Z	F
6	G	J	H
7	K	H	J

4. Write a month starting with each of the letters you hear

1.   5.

2.   6.

3.   7.

4.

5. Spot the intruder letter

a. Beattriz

b. Javiler

c. Maijte

d. Gabriella

e. Henrique

f. Alfonsio

g. Jeorge

h. Juliána

6. Listen and write the names being spelled out

1. _ _ _ _   4. _ _ _ _ _

2. _ _ _ _   5. _ _ _ _ _

3. _ _ _ _ _ _   6.* _ _ _ _   _ _ _ _ _ _

* "Espacio" means space

THE LANGUAGE GYM

UNIT 3 – DESCRIBING HAIR AND EYES

1. Fill in the blanks

a. Tengo _ _ pelo _ _ _ _ _ _ _ _ _ _

b. Mi hermano _ _ _ _ _ el pelo _ _ _ _ _ _

c. Tengo _ _ _ ojos _ _ _ _ _ _

d. Antonio _ _ _ _ _ el _ _ _ _ rubio y los ojos _ _ _ _ _ _

e. _ _ hermana _ _ _ _ _ gafas

f. Tengo _ _ _ _ _ _ corto y en _ _ _ _ _

g. Tengo los _ _ _ _ marrones y _ _ _ _ _ barba

2. Break the flow

a. Tengoelpelomorenoyliso

b. Tienelosojosazulesygrandes

c. Tieneelpelomorenoyamediamelena

d. Tieneelpelocastaño,largoyrizado

e. Notienepelo

f. Tienelosojosnegrosyllevagafas

g. Tienelosojosmarronesyllevabigote

3. Arrange in the correct order

Me llamo Fran	1
Tengo doce años	
Mi cumpleaños es el treinta de marzo	
Tengo el pelo moreno, liso y corto	
Soy de Valladolid en España	
Tiene el pelo rubio y los ojos verdes	
Él tiene quince años	
Su cumpleaños es el catorce de marzo	
Tengo un hermano	
Tengo los ojos negros	

4. Spot the intruders – Identify the word in each sentence the speaker is NOT saying

a. Tengo el pelo muy largo

b. Tengo el pelo a la media melena

c. Mi padre tiene el pelo bastante corto

d. Mi madre no tiene el pelo largo

e. Mi hermano menor tiene el pelo rubio

f. Mi hermana tiene el pelo moreno en punta

5. Listen, spot and correct the errors

a. Me llamo Serena

b. Tengo dieciséis años

c. Soy de Argentina

d. …pero vivo en Escocia

e. Tengo el pelo rubio y los ojos marrones

f. Tengo el pelo largo y ondulado

g. Mi mejor amiga, Kat, tiene catorce años

h. Es guapa. Tiene el pelo rubio, muy largo y liso

i. Tiene los ojos grises y lleva gafas

6. Fill in the blanks

a. Tengo el pelo en pun_______

b. Tengo el pelo casta_______

c. Tengo los ojos ne_______

d. Tengo el pelo lar_______

e. Tengo los ojos azu_______

f. No llevo ga_______

g. No llevo bigo_______

h. Llevo bar_______

i. Mi padre lle_____ bigote

j. Mi hermano tiene los ojos gri_____

7. Faulty translation: spot the translation errors and correct them

a. I am fourteen years old.

b. My birthday is on 14 June.

c. I have two brothers.

d. I have dark brown hair, long and curly.

e. I have blue eyes and wear glasses.

f. My older brother is called Paco. He is eighteen.

g. His birthday is on 20 July.

h. He has blond hair, short and wavy.

i. He has green eyes and wears glasses.

j. He has a moustache.

8. Spot the missing words and write them in

Me llamo Juan Miguel. Tengo pelo rubio, largo rizado y los ojos azules. Mi madre se llama Marta y mi padre llama Claudio. Mi madre tiene el pelo moreno, muy largo y ondulado, y ojos marrones. Mi es completamente calvo y tiene los ojos verdes. Tengo un hermano se llama Fernando. el pelo rubio, corto y rizado, y los ojos azules. Fernando lleva gafas. También tengo una novia se llama Patricia. Tiene el pelo pelirrojo, media melena y liso. Tiene los ojos verdes.

9. Listen, spot and correct the grammar/spelling errors

a. Me llama Miguel.

b. Tengo trece anos.

c. Tengo la pelo moreno, largo y liso.

d. Tengo azules ojos.

e. Llevo las gafas.

f. Mi hermano se llamo Pablo.

g. Tengo quatorce años.

h. Pablo tengo el pelo rubio, corto y rizado.

i. Tiene los negros ojos. No lleva gafas.

10. Listen and fill in the grid

	Hair	Eyes	Wears glasses
1. José			
2. Paco			
3. Nina			
4. Dylan			
5. Miguel			
6. Marta			

11. Translate the ten sentences you hear into English

1.

2.

3.

4.

5.

6.

7.

8.

9.

10.

12. Narrow listening - Gapped translation

My name is Veronica, I am ______________ years old. My birthday is on the______________ of

________________. In my family there are ______________ people: my father, my mother, my two

__________________ and me. My mother has __________ hair, __________ and curly. She has

__________ eyes. My father has grey hair, __________ and straight. He has __________ eyes. My two

sisters have __________ hair, long and straight. They both have ____________ eyes. I have brown,

__________________ hair. However, before, I used to have it ____________.

13. Listening slalom: follow the speaker from top to bottom and number the boxes accordingly

1 - Fran	2 - Alia	3 - Kevin	4 - Manuela	5 - Juan Carlos
My name is Fran (1)	My name is Alia	My name is Kevin	My name is Manuela	My name is Juan Carlos
I am from Valencia	**I am from Cádiz (1)**	I am from Barcelona	I am from Santander	I am from Granada
but live in Rome, Italy	but live in Paris, France	but live in Santiago, Chile	**but live in London, England (1)**	but live in Madrid, Spain
I have one brother	I have two brothers	**I am only child (1)**	I have one sister	I have one brother and one sister
I have blond hair	I have dark brown hair	I have red hair	I have dark brown hair	**I have brown hair (1)**
long and straight	short and spiky	**long and curly (1)**	Short and wavy	medium length and straight
I have blue eyes (1)	I have brown eyes	I have green eyes	I have grey eyes	I have blue eyes

14. Fill in the grid

Name	Age	Birthday	Siblings	Hair (3 details)	Eyes
1. Mario	12	13 August	one brother one sister	blond, short, curly	brown
2. Andrea		20 June		dark brown, long, wavy	
3. Andrés	16		two brothers		blue
4. Eugenio		8 March		dark brown, short, spiky	
5. Melania	11		one brother		brown
6. Alfonso		19 May		blond, short, curly	

1. What are their names? Listen to the recording and write the letters you hear

1. _ _ _ _ _ _ _

2. _ _ _ _ _ _

3. _ _ _ _ _ _

4. _ _ _ _ _ _ _ _

5. _ _ _ _ _ _ _

6. _ _ _ _ _ _ _ _ _

7. _ _ _ _ _ _ _ _ _ _ _

3. Match the rhyming pairs – write which number word rhymes with the words on the left. For an extra mark, write the word you hear too.

a. año	
b. ojo	
c. largo	**1 (amargo)**
d. rapado	
e. verdes	
f. vengo	
g. nueve	
h. liso	

5. Spot the errors

a. Me llamo Carlos.

b. Tengo doce años.

c. Tengo el pelo negro, liso y corto.

d. Tengo los ojos azules.

e. No llevo gafas.

f. Tengo una hermana.

g. Mi hermana se llama Luisa.

h. Luisa tiene catorce años.

i. Tiene el pelo rubio, largo y ondulado.

j. Tiene los ojos verdes.

2. Complete the words

a. casta__o

b. ri__ado

c. __erdes

d. me __ __ amo

e. o__os

f. cator__e

g. a__os

h. pelir__o__o

i. marron__s

j. liso__

4. Faulty echo – what was different the second time you heard the word?

a. castaño

b. verdes

c. catorce

d. liso

e. azules

f. me llamo

g. ojos

h. pelirrojo

i. once

6. Track the sounds – Listen and write down how many times you hear the sounds 'J/Ge/Gi' 'TH' and 'LL' in each of the descriptions below

J/G /X/	
Th sound /θ/	
Ll /Y/	

UNIT 4 – SAYING WHERE I LIVE AND AM FROM

1. Fill in the blanks

a. Hola. Me __________ David. Vivo en una __________ muy grande en el centro de la __________.

b. Buenos días. Me llamo Conchi. _____ de Madrid. _______ en un piso pequeño en las __________.

c. ¿Qué tal? _____ llamo Maya. Soy _____ Cádiz. Vivo en un __________ bonito en la costa.

d. Hola. Me llamo __________. Soy de Quito, en ________. Vivo en una casa muy _________ en la montaña.

e. Buenos _______. Me llamo Daniel, vivo en Buenos Aires, en ____________. Vivo en un edificio __________ en el centro de Buenos Aires.

f. __________. Me llamo Beatriz. Vivo en _______ casa grande pero un poco _______ en La Habana.

2. Multiple choice quiz: select the correct location

	a	b	c
1. Javier	Bilbao	Valencia	Granada
2. Samuel	Cartagena	Madrid	La Habana
3. Juan Pablo	Lima	Zaragoza	Cádiz
4. Paco	Santiago	Quito	Madrid
5. Selina	Madrid	Barcelona	Bilbao
6. Ariana	Gerona	Zaragoza	Málaga
7. Patricio	Lima	Bogotá	Santiago
8. Manuel	Barcelona	Montevideo	Marbella

3. Spot the intruders – Identify the words the speaker is NOT saying

Hola. Me llamo Jaime. Tengo un catorce años y vivo ya en La Habana, el la capital de Cuba. En mi familia somos hay cuatro personas: mis padres, mi hermana, mi hermano y yo. Mi hermano que se llama Benicio. Vivo en una la casa pequeña en el centro de La Habana. Mi casa es muy bonita.

4. Geographical mistakes: listen and correct

a. Me llamo Nina. Soy de Barcelona. Barcelona está en Aragón.

b. Me llamo Pedro. Soy de Santiago. Santiago está en Argentina.

c. Me llamo Consuelo. Soy de Madrid. Madrid está en Cataluña.

d. Me llamo Juan. Soy de Quito. Quito está en Perú.

e. Me llamo Jaime. Soy de La Habana. La Habana está en España.

f. Me llamo Ariana. Soy de Cartagena. Cartagena está en Venezuela.

5. Spelling challenge: which place names are being spelled out? Fill in the grid

1	
2	
3	
4	
5	
6	
7	

<table>
<tr><td>

6. Faulty translation: spot the translation errors and correct them

My name is Maya. I am from Peru. I am twelve. I live in Catalunya, a region in the south of Spain.

I have blond hair and green eyes. My hair is long and curly.

I live with my mother, Eugenia and my two brothers, Silvia and Paola, in a small flat in the centre of Barcelona. My flat is in an old building. It is beautiful.

My father lives in a small house in the mountains. His house is ugly and modern.

</td><td>

7. Spot the missing words and write them in

1. Vivo Bogotá, la capital Colombia. Bogotá es una ciudad hermosa. Vivo en un piso en un edificio moderno en el centro ciudad.

2. Vivo con mi familia en Málaga, una ciudad turística en el sur España. Vivo en casa moderna en las afueras de ciudad.

3. Vivo en Quito, la capital de Ecuador. Vivo allí con mi familia y perro. Vivo en un piso grande feo en un edificio.

4. Vivo en Valencia, España. Vivo en una casa grande y moderna en la costa.

</td></tr>
</table>

8. Complete the grid in English, as shown in the example (names are spelled out for you)

Name	Country	Type of accommodation	House/flat location	Two details about the house/flat
1. Ana	*Spain*	*House*	*Town centre*	*1. Ugly* *2. Big*
2.				
3.				
4.				
5.				
6.				
7.				
8.				

9. Narrow listening - Gapped translation

My name is Julian. I am ___________years old and my birthday is on _________ August. I ___________in Bilbao, in the Basque Country, in the ___________of Spain. I live in an ___________house in the ___________. I have two ___________, Maite and Silvia. Maite is very ___________ but a bit silly. Silvia is a bit ___________ but very ___________ and funny. My friend Rubén ___________ in Barcelona but he is from Bilbao like ___________. He lives in a modern ___________ in the ___________. He has a big dog called _________. He lives in a big and ___________ flat.

10. Listening slalom: follow the speaker from top to bottom and number the boxes accordingly

1	2	3	4	5
I live in Argentina, (1)	I am from Bolivia and	I am from Peru and	I am from Spain and	I am from Colombia and
I live in Málaga.	I live in Lima.	I live near La Paz.	I live in Bogotá.	**near Buenos Aires. (1)**
I am 12 and	**I am 15 and (1)**	I am 14 and	I am 16 and	I am 13 and
I live in a big house	I live in a small house	I live in a very small house	**I live in a small flat (1)**	I live in a flat
in a modern building. (1)	in an old building.	in the city centre.	near a lake.	on the coast.
I like my house	**My flat is ugly (1)**	My house	My flat is cosy	My house is pretty
and beautiful.	and spacious.	**but very big. (1)**	is modern.	because it is big.

11. Narrow listening: fill in the grid as shown in the example (Mario)

Name	Age	Birthday	Town	Accommodation	Location	Description
1. Mario	*14*	*20th May*	*Málaga*	*House*	*Coast*	*Big*
2. Felipe						
3. Andrés						
4. Eugenio						
5. Melania						
6. Paola						

1. Listen to the two pairs and explain the difference in pronunciation in your own words

English	Español
Cuba	Cuba
Argentina	Argentina
Andalusia	Andalucía
Barcelona	Barcelona
La Habana	La Habana
Chile	Chile
Cartagena	Cartagena
David	David

2. Complete the words

a. __entro

b. afuera__

c. Ar__entina

d. Andalu__ía

e. Bogot__

f. __uito

g. Catalu__a

h. Zarago__a

i. La __abana

j. edifi__io

3. Listen to the teacher spell out the names

1. _ _ _ _ _ _

2. _ _ _ _ _

3. _ _ _ _ _ _ _

4. _ _ _ _ _ _ _ _ _ _

5. _ _ _ _ _ _ _ _

6. _ _ _ _ _ _

7. _ _ _ _ _

8. _ _ _ _ _ _ _

4. Faulty echo

a. Soy de Gerona

b. Una casa pequeña

c. Un piso antiguo

d. Un edificio moderno

e. En el centro

f. Soy de La Habana

g. Soy de Argentina

h. Vivo en Cartagena

5. Spot the errors

a. Una casa pequeña

b. Un piso antiguo

c. Soy de La Habana

d. Vivo en Argentina

e. Vivo en el centro

f. Soy de Zaragoza

g. Vivo en Cartagena

h. Un edificio moderno

6. Track the sound – Listen and write down how many times you hear the sounds 'jota', 'ñ' and 'th' (as in think) in each of the descriptions below

	jota $/X/$	ñ $/NY/$	th $/\theta/$
1			
2			
3			

UNIT 5 – TALKING ABOUT MY FAMILY MEMBERS (AGE & RELATIONSHIPS)

1. Fill in the blanks

a. En mi _ _ _ _ _ _ _ hay _ _ _ _ _ personas

b. Mi abuelo tiene _ _ _ _ _ _ años

c. En _ _ familia _ _ _ seis _ _ _ _ _ _ _ _

d. Mi _ _ _ _ _ se llama _ _ _ _ _

e. Me _ _ _ _ _ bien con _ _ hermano _ _ _ _ _

f. Me _ _ _ _ _ _ _ _ _ con mi _ _ _ _ _

g. Me llevo _ _ _ bien _ _ _ mi _ _ _ _ _

2. Break the flow

a. Haycuatropersonasenmifamilia.

b. Mellevobienconmispadres.

c. Miabuelotieneochentaaaños.

d. Mitìotienecuarentaaaños.

e. MihermanomayorsellamaJuan.

f. Enmifamiliahaycincopersonas.

g. Mipadretienecuarentaydosaños.

3. Multiple choice quiz: select the correct age

	a	b	c
1. Jaime	40	50	60
2. Silvia	90	80	70
3. Juan	30	40	60
4. Pedro	60	70	100
5. Marina	36	46	56
6. Consuelo	65	85	95
7. Enrique	33	63	73
8. Pablo	71	21	41
9. Manuela	57	67	47

4. Spot the intruders - Identify the word(s) in each sentence the speaker is NOT saying

a. En mi familia hay cinco mil personas.

b. Mi tío Pedro tiene cuarenta y un años.

c. Me llevo muy bien con mis padres.

d. Mi primo Ian tiene como cincuenta años.

e. Mis abuelos maternos tienen ochenta años.

f. Yo me llevo fatal con mi primo José.

5. Listen, spot and correct the errors

a. Mi abuelo tiene ochenta y dos años.

b. Hay cinco personas en mi familia.

c. En mi familia hay cinco personas: mi madre, mi padre y mis tres hermanos.

d. ¿Cuántos años tiene tu hermana menor?

e. Mi tío tiene setenta años.

f. Me llevo bien con mis padres, especialmente con mi madre.

g. En mi familia hay cuatro personas.

6. Complete the words then write the number it refers to

a. (Example) **Och**enta y siete **(87)**

b. Nov _ _ _ _ y cinco

c. Veinti_ _ _

d. _ _ _ renta y tres

e. _ _ en

f. No_ _ _ _ _ y ocho

g. Cin_ _ _ _ _ _ y nueve

h. Se_ _ _ _ _ y cuatro

7. Faulty translation: spot the translation errors and correct them

a. My name is Juan Francisco. I am 16 years old.

b. I have blond and long hair.

c. I have green eyes.

d. In my family there are 4 people: my father, my mother, my cousin, my brother and I.

e. My father is 54, my mother is 34, my sister is 9 and my brother is 7.

f. My aunt and uncle are called Roberta and Rafa. My aunt is 51 years old and my uncle is 70.

g. My maternal grandparents are 80 years old.

h. My paternal grandfather is 76.

8. Spot and write in the missing words

a. llamo Dylan.

b. Soy España.

c. Tengo hermano.

d. Mi cumpleaños el veinte de marzo.

e. En mi familia cinco personas.

f. Hay mi padre, mi madre, mis hermanos y yo.

g. Yo tengo treinta siete años. Mi madre tiene sesenta y dos años y mi padre sesenta un años.

h. Mi hermano tiene cuarenta años y mi hermano tiene treinta y cinco años.

i. Me llevo bien mis padres.

9. Listen, spot and correct the errors

a. Me llama Rafa.

b. Soy quince años.

c. Mi cumpleaños el trece de mayo.

d. En mi familia es cuatro personas: mis padres, mi hermano mayor y mi.

e. Mi padre es cuarenta años.

f. Mi madre tiene cuarenta dos años.

g. Mi hermano mayor tiene veinte y uno años.

h. Llevo bien con mis padres.

i. Me llevo mal en mi hermano.

10. Fill in the table

	Father's age	Mother's age	Sibling's age
1. Alex	56	48	18
2. Paco	43		15
3. Nina		51	
4. Dylan	55		
5. Miguel		68	
6. Marta			10

11. Translate the ten sentences you hear into English

1.

2.

3.

4.

5.

6.

7.

8.

9.

10.

12. Narrow listening: gapped translation

My name is Paco. I am from _____________ . I am _______________ years old. My birthday is on _____________

_____________________ . I have ____________ , long and _______________ hair. I have ____________ eyes. In my

family there are _______________ people: my stepfather, my ____________ and my two sisters.

My older sister is _______________ years old. My younger sister is _______________ years old. I

_____________________ with my parents. My _____________ grandfather lives with us. He is

_______________ years old. I get along with him.

13. Listening slalom: follow the speaker from top to bottom and number the boxes accordingly

1 - Elena	2 - Felipe	3 - Maite	4 - Javier	5 - Juan
My name is Elena (1)	My name is Felipe	My name is Maite	My name is Javier	My name is Juan
I am 17	**I am 16 (1)**	I am 20	I am 11	I am 30
My birthday is on 25th October	My birthday is on 20th June	**My birthday is on 31st December (1)**	My birthday is on 15th March	My birthday is on 7th January
My mother is 50	**My mother is 48 (1)**	My mother is 44	My mother is 39	My mother is 62
My father is 49	My father is 43	My father is 53	My father is 64	**My father is 52 (1)**
My grandad is 81	My grandad is 75	**My grandad is 76 (1)**	My grandad is 73	My grandad is 90
My grandma is 68 (1)	My grandma is 80	My grandma is 81	My grandma is 72	My grandma is 79

14. Narrow listening: listen and fill in the missing details on the grid

Name	Age	Birthday	Family size	Older sibling's age	Mother's age	Father's age
1. Andrea		20th June		16		41
2. Felipe	14		4			44
3. Sofía		15th Sept			43	
4. Eugenio	13		5		39	
5. Myriam	28			31		55

1. Complete with the missing letters

a. En m__ familia __ay cuatro persona__

b. M__ llevo bien co__ mi __ermano

c. Mi __ermana ma__or se llama Eu__enia

d. Mi tía Re__ina es muy __enerosa

e. Mi tío __uan es muy inteli__ente

f. Mi __ermana m__nor es di__ertida

g. Mi amiga An__ela es muy __abladora

h. Mi me__or ami__o se llama __or__e

i. M__ llevo mu__ bien con m__ padre

2. Listen to the lists below. What differences do you notice between the way 'G' is pronounced in the words in column A and B

	A	B
1	generoso	gordo
2	inteligente	delgado
3	Regina	guapo
4	Giraldo	Guillermo
5	geografía	gorra
6	Girona	Gandía

3. Write out each word below exactly as YOU hear it. How do you interpret the sounds?

a. hermano =

b. divertida =

c. mejor =

d. me =

e. mayor =

f. generoso =

g. bajo=

h. Regina =

4. Faulty echo

a. Mi hermano mayor

b. Mi hermano menor

c. Me llevo bien

d. Soy baja

e. Mi madre es generosa

f. En mi familia hay cuatro personas

g. Mi hermana es inteligente

h. Mi mejor amigo

5. Listen and rewrite the phrases below correctly based on what you hear

a. Soy baio = soy bajo

b. Mi hermano minor = ___________________

c. Me padre = ___________________

d. Soy inteligent = ___________________

e. Me levo bien = ___________________

f. En mi familia hey = ___________________

g. Mi hermano mejor = ___________________

6. Dictation – write out the sentences

a. ___________________

b. ___________________

c. ___________________

d. ___________________

e. ___________________

f. ___________________

g. ___________________

THE LANGUAGE GYM

1. Multiple choice quiz – select which adjective you hear

		a	b	c
1	**My father is…**	generous	fun	muscular
2	**My mother is…**	fat	intelligent	thin
3	**My older sister is…**	stupid	fat	muscular
4	**My younger sister is…**	tall	short	pretty
5	**My brother is…**	ugly	unfriendly	friendly
6	**My cousin Pablo is…**	big	strong	small
7	**My cousin Marta is…**	lazy	bad	boring
8	**My grandad is…**	mean	stubborn	annoying
9	**My grandma is…**	generous	good	fun
10	**My boyfriend is…**	patient	fat	muscular

2. Split sentences: listen and match

1. Jaime	a. Fun
2. Silvia	b. Boring
3. Juan	c. Short
4. Pedro	d. Tall
5. Marina	e. Good-looking
6. Consuelo	**f. Bad**
7. Enrique	g. Muscular
8. Pablo	h. Ugly
9. Paola	i. Stubborn
10. Manolo	j. Strong

3. Spot the intruders - Identify the word in each sentence the speaker is NOT saying

a. Mi hermano es muy guapo.

b. Mi tío Pedro tiene cuarenta y un años. Es bastante divertido.

c. Me llevo muy bien con mi padre porque es paciente y generoso.

d. Mi primo Ian no es muy alto.

e. Mi padre es de la estatura media.

f. Mi novia es demasiado habladora.

g. Yo soy alto, musculoso y fuerte.

4. Spot the differences and correct your text

a. Mi abuela es muy paciente.

b. Mi madre es muy inteligente.

c. En mi familia hay cinco personas: mi madre, mi padre, mis dos hermanos y yo.

d. ¿Cómo estás?

e. Mi tío tiene sesenta años pero es muy aburrido.

f. Me llevo mal con mis padres, especialmente con mi madre porque es muy antipática.

g. En mi familia somos todos bajos.

5. Categories - Listen to the words below and classify them in positive and negative

ADJETIVOS POSITIVOS	ADJETIVOS NEGATIVOS

6. Faulty translation: spot and correct the translation errors

a. My name is Juan Pablo. I am 16 years old. I have dark brown hair and green eyes. I am tall, muscular and quite good-looking. I am friendly, talkative and quite generous.

b. My mother is called Paola. She is fifty years old. She is short, slim and very funny. She is generous but a bit mean.

c. My father is called Roberto. He is 62 years old. He is neither tall nor short. He is quite clever. He is very generous, fun and patient.

d. My sister is called Carmen. She is 17. She is quite tall and slim. She is unfriendly and boring. She is also quite stupid and lazy.

8. Listen and complete with the correct masculine or feminine ending

a. Es muy simpátic__.

b. Son muy terc__ __.

c. Mi madre y mi padre son muy alt__ __.

d. Soy baj__ y pacient__.

e. ¡Qué gracios__ eres!

f. ¡Qué mal__ __ son!

g. Sus hij__ __ son muy gord__ __.

h. Mis herman__ __ son muy trabajador__ __.

i. ¡Qué divertid__ eres!

7. Spot the missing words and write them in

a. Me llamo Dylan y muy trabajador

b. Mi hermano es perezoso

c. Mi madre es terca antipática

d. Mi hermano es de media

e. Mis padres muy buenos

f. Mi hermana es muy generosa

g. Detesto mi primo porque es terco

9. Listen and fill in the grid

Person	Description
1. My father is	
2. My mother is	
3. My sister is	
4. My brother is	
5. My cousin Pablo is	
6. My cousin Marta is	
7. My grandfather is	
8. My grandmother is	
9. My best friend is	

10. Translate the ten sentences you hear into English

1.

2.

3.

4.

5.

6.

7.

8.

9.

10.

11. Narrow listening: gapped translation

My name is Pablo. I love my parents. They are a bit ___________, but very generous, _________ and hard-working. I have ___________ brothers and one sister. My older brother is very annoying: he is ___________, lazy, ___________ and very talkative.

My younger brother is lovely: he is nice, ______________, patient, ______________, hard-working and helpful. My sister is pretty and very______________, but very boring. I also have a ______________. Her name is Pilar. She is tall, ________________, pretty and is very ______________.

12. Listening slalom: follow the speaker from top to bottom and number the boxes accordingly

1 - Nina	2 - Kevin	3 - Manuela	4 - Juan Carlos	5 - Ana
My name is Nina (1)	My name is Kevin	My name is Manuela	My name is Juan Carlos	My name is Ana
I am 15 years old	**I am 17 years old (1)**	I am 18 years old	I am 13 years old	I am 12 years old
I am tall and fat	I am neither tall nor short	**I am tall and slim (1)**	I am not very tall	I am short and slim
My older brother is short and slim	My older sister is short and slim	My younger brother is short and slim	My older sister is short and very pretty	**My younger brother is tall and strong (1)**
I love her	I get along very well with him	I like her a lot	**I get along with him (1)**	I don't get along with him
because he is nice and positive	because she is generous	because he is mean	because she is fun	**because he is patient and helpful. (1)**
and kind.	Also, he is very funny.	**Also, he is very generous and kind. (1)**	and funny.	and stubborn.

13. Narrow listening: fill in the grid

Name	Name of older sibling	Age of older sibling	Birthday of older sibling	Character of older sibling	Appearance of older sibling
1. Felipe					
2. Andrea					
3. Eugenio					
4. Melania					

1. Multiple choice quiz

		a	b	c
1	At home we have…	four pets	two pets	five pets
2	I have a…	turtle	dog	cat
3	My brother has a…	turtle	fish	parrot
4	My older sister has a…	lizard	rabbit	duck
5	My younger sister has a…	mouse	fish	horse
6	My mother has a…	cat	dog	parrot
7	My father has a…	bird	horse	dog
8	My grandparents have two…	dogs	horses	rabbits
9	My best friend has a…	lizard	dog	snake
10	My girlfriend has a…	fish	cat	dog

2. Split sentences - listen and match

1. Arantxa	a. A dog
2. Silvia	b. A rabbit
3. Consuelo	c. A parrot
4. Juan	d. A fish
5. Felipe	e. A cat
6. Paco	f. A horse
7. Julio	g. Two dogs
8. Verónica	h. Two turtles
9. Roberto	i. Two mice
10. Simona	j. A mouse

3. Spot the intruders - Identify the word in each sentence the speaker is not saying

a. Mi hermano tiene un gran perro.

b. Mi mejor amiga no tiene dos mascotas.

c. Mis abuelos tienen dos caballos.

d. La tortuga verde de mi hermano se llama Peggy.

e. Mi novia tiene un perro blanco.

f. Mi perro marrón es mono pero un poco feo.

g. Tengo dos peces naranjas.

4. Spot the differences and correct your text

a. Mi perro es muy mono.

b. Mi gato es muy inteligente.

c. Tenemos cuatro mascotas: un perro, un gato, un loro y un pez dorado.

d. ¿Tienes un hámster?

e. Mi tío tiene un ratón y una serpiente en casa.

f. Mi hermana tiene una cobaya muy gorda.

g. Tenemos dos perros y un caballo en casa.

h. ¡Paco tiene una araña negra muy grande en casa!

5. Categories - Listen to the sentences and write in any adjectives or nouns you hear into the table

NOMBRES (Nouns)	ADJETIVOS (Adjectives)

THE LANGUAGE GYM

6. Spot the missing words and write them in

Me llamo Juan. Tengo mascotas: un perro se llama Rufus, una gata que llama Nairobi y serpiente que se llama María.

Rufus tres años. Es negro y blanco. Es gordo y tranquilo. Nairobi es atigrada y traviesa. Tiene los ojos verdes grandes. Es inteligente pero aburrida. Tiene cuatro años. María es una serpiente muy grande. Tiene un año.

7. Fill in the blanks

En casa tenemos tres ______________: un perro, un __________ y una ___________. Mi perro se _________ Eduardo. Es _________. Me encanta porque es muy _________ y __________.
Mi conejo se llama Zanahoria. Es ________ y ___________. Es muy ________ y ______. Mi rata se llama Ramona. Es __________ y blanca. Es muy inteligente y ___________. ¡Me encanta!

8. Faulty translation: correct the translation

My name is Roberto I am fifteen years old and live in Malaga. In my family there are three people: my parents, my older brother, Juan and myself. Juan is twelve years old and is very boring. We have three pets: a parrot who is called Leo, a cat who is called Tito and a lizard who is called Ágata. Leo is very talkative. Tito is fat and Ágata is boring, just like my brother.

9. Listen and fill in the grid

	Description
My father is	
My mother is	
My sister is	
My brother is	
My cousin Pablo is	
My cousin Marta is	
My grandad is	
My grandma is	

10. Translate the sentences into English

1.

2.

3.

4.

5.

6.

7.

8.

9.

11. Sentence puzzle - rewrite correctly

a. una rata Tengo gris, un conejo marrón muy blanco y un gato.

b. Gordo gato llama se Mi come muchísimo porque.

c. Mi tiene una serpiente verde que muy grande, negra amigo Pablo y se llama Veneno

d. una Tenemos tortuga llama Pilar y un ratón marrón verde que se que se llama Pedro.

12. Narrow listening - Gapped translation

My name is ___________. I am ___________ years old and _________ in _________. In my family there are ___________ people: my ___________, my mother, my ___________ brother, my ___________ and I. We have a few ___________. First, we have a ___________ dog called Maximus. He is ___________ and beautiful. He is very ___________ and eats ___________. We also have a ___________ called Leonardo. My turtle is small, green and ___________. She is very quiet and fun. Finally, we have a ___________ called Charlie. He is very ___________ and funny. He is red, ___________ and ___________. I love my ___________.

13. Listening slalom: follow the speaker from top to bottom and number the boxes accordingly

1	2	3	4	5
We have three (1)	I have	My friend has	My grandparents have	My friend has
four pets at home.	**pets at home. (1)**	five pets at home.	six pets at home.	one pet at home.
A blue fish,	Two big black dogs	**A green turtle (1)**	A big fat cat	Three fat, white guinea pigs
He is black and white	a big brown dog	a beautiful yellow bird,	**very slow and funny, (1)**	a yellow parrot
which is talkative and funny	**a cute and fat dog (1)**	a very fat duck	a cute guinea pig and	He is very lazy
and boring.	and a very cute black rabbit.	**and a gold fish. (1)**	a fun white mouse.	and two pretty Siamese cats.

14. Narrow listening: fill in the grid

Name	Age	Physical	Character	Type of pet	Pet description (3 details)
1. Juan Carlos					
2. Marisa					
3. Pedro					
4. Elena					

1. Multiple choice quiz: select the correct job

	1	2	3
1. Eva	accountant	nurse	housewife
2. Rosa	lawyer	farmer	mechanic
3. Pablo	engineer	businessman	doctor
4. Pau	househusband	singer	cook
5. Ada	waitress	receptionist	policeman
6. Ana	farmer	actress	doctor
7. Marta	teacher	astronaut	postman
8. Sam	lawyer	labourer	mechanic
9. Teo	househusband	singer	cook
10. Lea	student	doctor	farmer

2. Listening for detail: Did you hear the masculine or the feminine form?

	MASCULINE	FEMININE
1	actor	actriz
2	cocinero	cocinera
3	hombre de negocios	mujer de negocios
4	granjero	granjera
5	ingeniero	ingeniera
6	abogado	abogada
7	aburrido	aburrida
8	activo	activa
9	divertido	divertida

3. Split sentences - Listen and match

1. Iván	a. Labourer
2. Silvia	b. Lawyer
3. Paco	c. Doctor
4. Felipe	d. Cook
5. Consuelo	e. Accountant
6. Juan	f. Hairdresser
7. Verónica	g. Teacher
8. Julio	h. Mechanic
9. Roberto	i. Footballer
10. Maite	**j. Actor**

4. Spot the intruders: identify the words the speaker is NOT saying

Me llamo Juan Carlos y voy a hablarte de mi familia. En mi familia somos tres personas: mi padre, mi madre, mi hermano y yo. Mi padre se llama Pablo. Tiene cincuenta y seis años. Es muy alto y un poco gordo. Es calvo. Es simpático y también es trabajador. Trabaja como un contable. No le gusta porque es un trabajo bien pagado. Mi madre trabaja como una peluquera. Le encanta este trabajo porque él es muy divertido y gratificante. A mí me gustaría trabajar como un cocinero y ser famoso como Gordon Ramsay.

5. Listen, spot and correct the errors

Me llamo Mario. Soy de Bilbao. Mi persona favorita en mi familia es mi madre. Es tímida pero muy simpática. Mi madre es contable pero ahora no trabaja. Odio a mi padre. Es inteligente pero muy muy antipático. Mi padre es mecánico pero odia su trabajo porque es difícil y aburrido. Trabaja en un garaje en Bilbao. En casa tengo una cobaya que se llama Donatello. Es lenta pero muy graciosa, como mi hermana Casandra.

6. Categories - Listen to the six sentences and classify the words you hear in adjectives and nouns

NOMBRES (Nouns)	ADJETIVOS (Adjectives)

7. Spot the missing words and write them in

Me llamo Maite. En mi familia cuatro personas. Mi padre se llama Emilio y abogado. gusta su trabajo porque es estimulante. Sin embargo, es estresante. Mi madre es ama casa y le gusta bastante trabajo. Dice es muy gratificante. En casa tengo un perro se llama Corona. ¡Es muy y! No me gustan los gatos.

8. Faulty translation - correct the errors

My name is Felipe. I am twenty years old and live in Cartagena, in Colombia. In my family there are four people. I have a very funny dog called Johnny. My father works as a cook in a restaurant in the town centre. He does not like his job because it is stressful. My mother is a doctor. She likes her job a lot because it is rewarding and easy.

9. Listen and fill in the grid

Person	Job
My father	
My mother	
My older brother	
My younger brother	
My sister	
My best friend	
My girlfriend	
My grandad	

10. Translate the sentences into English

1.

2.

3.

4.

5.

6.

7.

8.

9.

11. Listen, spot and correct the errors

a. Yo trabaja en el campo.

b. Mi madre trabajan como cocinera.

c. Mi padre soy peluquero.

d. Mis hermanos no trabajamos.

e. Mi novia es actor.

f. Mi mejor amigo bomber.

g. Mi prima es médico.

h. Mis tios son granjero.

12. Narrow listening - Gapped translation

My name is ________________. In my family there are _________ people. My ________________ is called
Cristián. He is tall and ________________. He works as a ________________. He loves his job because it is
________________. My mother is an ________________.

She does not __________ her job because it is ____________. She wants to be a ____________ because it is
very ________________and she is very ____________. My two ____________ are students at
________________. They love it because it is ____________ and ____________. I am still a ________________
in a secondary school. I hate school because it is ____________ and ________________.

13. Listening Comprehension – listen and answer the questions about Valeria and Fernando

TEXT 1: Valeria		TEXT 2: Fernando	
Her father's job:		His father's job:	
What does her dad think about his job?		What does his dad think about his job?	
What job does Valeria's mother do?		What job does his mother do?	
What does her mum think about her job?		What does his mum think about her job?	
What job does Valeria want to do one day?		What job does Fernando want to do one day?	
Why?		Why?	

14. Fill in the grid

Name	Age	Character and physique	Father's job	Mother's job	His/her ideal job
Juan Carlos					
Marisa					
Pedro					
Andrea					

1. Multiple choice quiz: select the correct adjective

	1	2	3
1. Alex	boring	tall	friendly
2. Rosa	short	unfriendly	young
3. Pablo	hard-working	noisy	relaxed
4. Paco	fat	slim	good-looking
5. Ada	strong	lazy	stupid
6. Pepe	short	unfriendly	young
7. Marta	strong	fat	stupid
8. Sam	slim	lazy	friendly
9. Teo	strong	sporty	serious
10. Lea	hard-working	noisy	lazy

2. Listening for detail: Did you hear the masculine or the feminine form?

MASCULINE	FEMININE
aburrido	aburrida
hablador	habladora
perezoso	perezosa
ruidoso	ruidosa
tranquilo	tranquila
alto	alta
simpático	simpática
serio	seria
trabajador	trabajadora

3. Complete with 'más…que', 'menos…que' or 'tan…como' as shown in the example

a. (example) Mi madre es **más** alta **que** mi padre.

b. Mi hermano es _______ deportista _______ yo.

c. Mi gato es _______ tranquilo _______ mi perro.

d. Yo soy _______ fuerte _______ mi primo.

e. Mi abuelo es _______ viejo _______ mi abuela.

f. Mi mejor amigo es _______ bajo _______ yo.

g. Mi tío es _______ gordo _______ mi padre.

h. Mi primo Ian es _______ guapo _______ mi primo Ronnie.

5. Spot the differences and correct your text

a. Yo soy más alto que mi madre.

b. Mi primo es tan perezoso como yo.

c. Mi mejor amigo es más trabajador que yo.

d. Mi hermana es menos guapa que mi madre.

e. Mi perro es más ruidoso que mi pato.

f. Mi abuela es menos vieja que mi abuelo.

g. Mi madre es tan deportista como mi hermano y yo.

4. Listen and fill in the middle column with the missing information in English.

e.g. Arantxa is taller than Felipe.

1. Silvia		**Alfonso**
2. Juan		**Pedro**
3. Paco		**Jaime**
4. Maite		**Gonzalo**
5. Consuelo		**Pilar**
6. Julio		**Yolanda**
7. Felipe		**Jordi**
8. Dylan		**Samuel**
9. Verónica		**Sergio**

6. Spot the missing words and write them in

Me llamo Jaime. En mi familia tres personas. Somos deportistas, pero mis padres son más deportistas que yo.

Somos todos altos, pero yo soy más alto mis padres. Somos todos poco gordos, pero mi padre es más gordo

que madre y yo. ¡ soy el más delgado de mi familia! Somos todos trabajadores, pero mis padres son más

trabajadores que yo. Yo soy un perezoso.

7. Faulty translation: spot the translation errors and correct them

My name is Juan Francisco. In my family there

are two people: my father, my granny and I. We

are all very slim but I am slimmer than my

parents. We are all funny, but my mother and I are

more clever and quieter than my father. We are all

short, but my father and my stepfather are taller

than me. I am the silliest in the family.

9. Listen, spot and correct the errors

a. Mi madre es más alto como yo.

b. Mi padre es más trabajador que mi.

c. Mi hermano mayor soy más fuerte que mi

hermano menor.

d. Mi abuelo es más vieja que mi abuela.

e. Yo soy más delgado de mis padres.

f. Mis tíos son muy más viejos que mis padres.

g. Mis abuelos maternos son tan viejo como mis

paternos abuelos.

h. Mis primos es más ricos que nuestros.

8. Listen and complete the translation

Person	Description
1. My father is…	
2. My mother is…	
3. My older brother is…	
4. My younger brother is…	
5. My sister is…	
6. My uncle is…	
7. My grandma is…	
8. My best friend is….	
9. My girlfriend is…	
10. My dog is…	

10. Narrow listening - Gapped translation

My name is Antonio. I am _______________ years old. I am from Mérida, but live in __________. In my family

we are __________ people: my parents, my two _________, Carlos, Luis, and me. Carlos is _________, more

handsome and __________ than Luis, but Luis is friendlier, more intelligent and _____________ than Carlos.

My __________ are called Fernando and Pilar. Both are very _________ but my father is ___________ than my

mother. Moreover, my mother is more patient and less stubborn than my father. I am as ____________ as my

father! I have a pet, a ____________ called Amo. My parents say Amo is as ___________ as me.

11. Listen and write down what order you hear each chunk of text

	My father is funnier than my mother
	Gabriela is prettier than Consuelo
	I am as fun as my mother
1	**My name is Pilar.**
	…but Consuelo is much nicer than Gabriela
	…but my father is less fun than my mother
	I am twenty years old
	However, my dog is as lazy as a sloth.
	I live with my parents and two sisters, Gabriela and Consuelo

12. Answer the questions below about Enrique

a. How old is he?

b. Where does he live?

c. How many people are there in the family?

d. Pablo is________________ and ________________ than Julio.

e. Julio is ________________ and ________________than Pablo.

f. Why does he prefer his father?

g. He is as ________________ as his mother.

h. Which of his pets is more talkative?

13. Listening slalom: follow the speaker from top to bottom and number the boxes accordingly

1	2	3	4
My mother is more (1)	My mother is as	My mother is less	My stepmother is
affectionate than my father,	**talkative than my father, (1)**	less hard working than my mother	hardworking as my father,
as sporty as	as lazy as	**as tall as (1)**	less generous than
my father	I	my older sister	**my younger sister (1)**
and less	and much more	**and more (1)**	and as
boring	**annoying (1)**	unfriendly	intelligent than
as my younger sister	her sisters	than my goldfish.	**than my brother (1)**

1. Multiple choice quiz - What items do they have?

	a	b	c
1. Rafa	a red pen	a red pencil	a red rubber
2. Alejandra	a modern computer	modern furniture	a modern classroom
3. Rocco	three books	three pencil sharpeners	three felt tip pens
4. Gabriela	a blue rubber	a blue textbook	a blue pen
5. José Luis	some grey pencils	some blue pencils	some green pencils
6. Dylan	a black pencil case	a black textbook	a black rubber
7. María Elena	an orange pencil sharpener	an orange felt-tip pen	an orange rubber
8. Teodoro	a red exercise book	a red pencil	a red ruler
9. Consuelo	a white ruler	a white schoolbag	a white dictionary

2. Fill in the blanks

a. En mi ___________ tengo dos lápices.

b. En mi ___________ hay dos ____________.

c. Me hace ____________ un ____________.

d. Mi ___________ Paco no ____________ una goma.

e. No tengo ni ___________ ni _____________.

f. En mi ____________ hay un _____________ dos

____________ y tres _____________.

g. En mi _____________ hay una _____________ del

profesor y _____________ pupitres (desks).

3. Listening for detail: tick which items the speaker does NOT have

1. Arantxa	a red pencil case
	two pens
	a glue stick
	a pencil sharpener
	a pencil
	six felt-tip pens
2. Silvia	a green pencil case
	felt-tip pens
	two glue sticks
	three books
	a black pencil
	a white rubber
3. Vero	a calculator
	a red ruler
	two books
	two pencils
	a rubber
	a fountain pen

4. Spot the differences and correct your text

a. En mi mochila hay un estuche rojo, un libro de matemáticas, un libro de geografía, dos cuadernos azules, un bolígrafo y un portátil (laptop).

b. Mi amigo Carlos tiene unos rotuladores, unos bolígrafos, un sacapuntas, una pluma, unos rotuladores y un compás en su estuche. No tiene una agenda. No tiene una calculadora tampoco.

c. Mi amiga Consuelo tiene un estuche verde. En su estuche tiene dos reglas, un rotulador, una regla y un compás.

6. Faulty translation: spot and correct the errors

My name is Antonio. I am 14 years old and live in Valencia, in Portugal. In my family there are five people. My father, my mother, my brother my sister and I. We have a very funny duck too. In my classroom there are many chairs. There is a whiteboard, a piano and twenty desks. My classroom is very small. In my schoolbag I have a blue pen, a yellow compass, a new rubber and a white exercise book. My friend Marco has pens of all colours. Incredible!

7. What do José Luis and his friends need? Please also write the colour if it is mentioned

Person	Item
1. I (José Luis) need…	
2. My brother needs…	
3. Silvia needs…	
4. Nina needs…	
5. Pilar needs…	
6. Conchi needs…	
7. Rafa needs…	
8. Miguel needs…	
9. Rocío needs…	
10. Teresa needs…	

8. Listen, spot and correct the errors

a. Me hace falta una bolígrafo.

b. Mi amigo Paco tiene ocho lápiz.

c. Tengo un mochila blanco y dos gomas.

d. Mi clase pequeña pero bonita.

e. Tenemos una mascota mi clase, una cobaya.

f. En mi estuche tengo dos regla.

g. A mi hermana hace falta un ordenador.

h. Mis primos no tienen nada. Le hace falta todo.

9. Narrow listening - Gapped translation (HINT: Be careful with word order!)

My name is Simona and I am ______________. I am ______________ years old and I live in the ______________ of Italy. In my family there are ______________ people. I have a white ______________ and a black ______________. In my ______________ I have a lot of things. I have a green ______________, a yellow ______________, a white ______________, a grey ______________ and a white and blue ______________. The rubber is my favourite. My ______________ is very big and ______________. My best friend ______________ Lucía. She has only got one ______________ in her pencil case: a ______________. In her house she has a pet. It is a ______________, yellow and blue ______________ which speaks and sings.

<table>
<tr><td colspan="2">

10. Listen and arrange the information in the same order as it occurs in the text

	I don't get along with my stepfather.
	In my family there are four people.
	I like my school.
1	**My name is Alejandra.**
	I love my mother.
	But in my classroom there isn't a computer.
	I am twelve and live in Alicante.
	I have a brand new school bag.
	Alicante is in the southeast of Spain.
	…and I carry many things inside.

</td><td>

11. Answer the questions below about Enrique

a. Who is his favourite brother?

b. What does his father do for a living? And his mother?

c. What does he say about his school?

d. Why does he not like his classroom?

e. What 3 (different) things are there in his schoolbag?

f. What two things does he not have?

</td></tr>
</table>

12. Listening slalom: follow the speaker from top to bottom and number the boxes accordingly

1	2	3	4
In my pencil case (1)	In his schoolbag	In my schoolbag	In her pencil case
there are	my sister has	**I only have (1)**	my brother has
a diary	many things.	a few pencils	**a pen (1)**
a few felt tip pens	**a pencil (1)**	there are two books	a pencil case
some exercise books	**a rubber (1)**	a calculator	three exercise books
a pencil sharpener (1)	a ruler	a red pencil case	a dictionary
and two pens	and a computer	and his tablet	**and scissors (1)**

1. Listen and 'shadow' the speaker by whispering after them, focusing on the letters underlined. Then read the text aloud to yourself.

Me llamo Pablo. Me encantan mis padres. Son un poco estrictos, pero muy generosos, amables y trabajadores. Tengo dos hermanos y una hermana. Mi hermano mayor es muy molesto: es ruidoso, perezoso, antipático, y muy hablador. Mi hermano menor es un encanto: es simpático, generoso, paciente, servicial y trabajador. Mi hermana es guapa y muy inteligente, pero muy aburrida. También tengo una novia. Se llama Pilar. Es alta, interesante, guapa y es muy graciosa.

2. Listen and 'shadow' the speaker - focusing on the letters underlined

Me llamo Dylan. Tengo trece años y vivo en Londres. En mi familia hay cinco personas: mi padrastro, mi madre, mi hermano mayor, mi hermanastra y yo. Tenemos algunas mascotas. Primero, tenemos un perro enorme que se llama Maximus. Es negro y hermoso. Es muy fuerte y come mucho. También tenemos una tortuga que se llama Leonardo. Mi tortuga es pequeña, verde y graciosa. Es muy tranquila y divertida. Finalmente, tenemos un loro que se llama Charlie. Él es muy hablador y gracioso. Es rojo, azul y amarillo. Me encantan mis mascotas.

3. Read the text below silently, then underline every 'c' and 'qu' pronounced 'K' like the 'C' in 'cake' and all the 'c' and 'z' pronounced like 'TH' in 'think. Then listen to see if you got it right

Me llamo Carmen y tengo veinte años. Soy de Zaragoza, pero vivo en Valencia. En mi familia somos cinco personas: mis padres, mis dos hermanos, Carlos y Marcelo, y yo. Carlos es más alto, más guapo y más fuerte que Marcelo, pero Marcelo es más amable, más paciente y trabajador que Carlos. Mis padres se llaman Fernando y Mercedes. Ambos son muy simpáticos pero mi padre es más estricto que mi madre. Además, mi madre es más paciente y menos terca que mi padre. ¡Yo soy tan terca como mi padre! Tengo una mascota, un conejo que se llama Amo. Mis padres dicen que Amo es tan perezoso como yo.

4. Listen and 'shadow' the speaker - focusing on the words underlined

Me llamo Antonio. Tengo 15 años y vivo en Cádiz, en España. En mi familia hay cinco personas. Mi padrastro, mi madre, mi hermano, mi hermanastra y yo. También tenemos una cobaya muy graciosa. En mi clase hay muchas cosas. Hay una pizarra, un ordenador y treinta escritorios. Mi clase es muy grande. En mi estuche tengo un lápiz azul, un rotulador amarillo, una goma nueva y una regla blanca. Mi amigo Marco tiene lápices de todos los colores.

5. Listen and 'shadow' the speaker - focusing on the words underlined

Me llamo Simona y soy asturiana. Tengo 14 años y vivo en el sur de Italia. En mi familia hay seis personas. Tengo un gato blanco y un conejo negro. En mi estuche hay muchas cosas. Tengo un bolígrafo verde, un rotulador amarillo, una regla blanca, un compás gris y una goma blanca y azul. La goma es mi favorita. Mi mochila es muy grande y bonita. Mi mejor amiga se llama Lucía. Ella solo tiene una cosa en su estuche: un bolígrafo. En su casa tiene una mascota. Es un loro grande, amarillo y azul que habla y canta.

1. Listen and fill in the gaps

a. Me encanta el ____________________ .

b. A Rafa le gusta mucho la ____________________ .

c. A Paco no le gustan nada las ____________________ .

d. A Alejandro le gusta muchísimo el ____________________ .

e. A mi padre le encanta la ______________ de fresa.

f. Mi madre odia los ____________________ .

g. A mi hermano le encantan los ____________________ .

h. A mi hermana le chifla el ____________ ____________ picante.

i. Odio los ____________________ .

2. Mystery words – guess the words, then listen and see how many you guessed right.

a. el a__ __ a

b. la m __e __

c. el __u__ v __

d. la __ a __n__

e. el p __ __ c__ __ __

f. la m __ __ z __ __ __

g. el __ __ n

h. el __ r __ __ z

3. Listening for detail: tick which food items Marta and Sergio usually eat for breakfast

Marta	Mantequilla
	Pan tostado
	Zumo de fruta
	Mermelada
	Un huevo
	Queso
	Un café con leche
Sergio	Una salchicha
	Un huevo
	Arroz
	Un café
	Pan con miel
	Zumo de naranja
	Un plátano

4. Spot the differences and correct your text

a. Me encanta la fruta, sobre todo las moras.

b. Odio las verduras, sobre todo los champiñones.

c. No me gusta el pollo frito.

d. Me gusta muchisímo el marisco.

e. Me gusta mucho la pasta.

f. Me encanta el zumo de manzana.

g. La carne roja es sana.

h. El café es sabroso.

i. Las hamburguesas son sanas.

j. Las verduras son sabrosas.

k. Las manzanas son crujientes.

l. No me gusta mucho la leche.

5. Spot the missing words and write them in

Me llamo Fernando ¿Qué comer? Me encanta marisco, entonces me gustan las gambas porque son deliciosos.

Me encanta el pescado porque sabroso y rico proteínas. Me encanta el salmón. Me gusta el pollo asado

picante. Me gusta mucho la fruta, sobre todo los plátanos. No aguanto las verduras porque asquerosas.

6. Faulty translation: spot the translation errors and correct them

My name is Felipe. What do I enjoy eating? I love

fruit, especially bananas. I drink them every day.

My favourite vegetables are tomatoes and potatoes

because they are healthy. I also like jam because it

is delicious and meat because it is tasty. I hate

turkey and burgers. They are rich in protein but

they are not spicy.

8. Listen, spot and correct the spelling and grammar errors

a. Me gusta las verduras porque son sanas.

b. Me encanta las hamburguesas.

c. El pescado y la carne son sabrosas.

d. Me gustan bastante el zumo de naranja.

e. Como muy pescado porque es rico en proteínas.

f. No me gusta carne porque es grasienta.

g. Me encanta la pollo asado porque es sabroso.

h. Me gusta mucho los calamares fritos aunque sean malsanos.

7. Why do they like/dislike these foods?

People and what they like/dislike	Reasons why they like/dislike
1. I like fruit	
2. My brother loves eggs	
3. Silvia hates vegetables	
4. Nina dislikes churros	
5. Jaime likes fish	
6. Conchi loves oranges	
7. Rafa loves Indian food	
8. Ahmed dislikes pork	
9. Rocio dislikes sausages	
10. Pilar dislikes tomatoes	
11. Teresa hates french fries	
12. Susana hates carrots	

9. Narrow listening - Gapped translation

My name is Julián. What do I like to eat? Well, I prefer ______________, especially ______________. I love it

because it is ______________. I like burgers ______________. I love ______________ too. I eat them with

______________. I also like fruit a lot because it is ______________. I don't like ______________. I hate tomatoes

and ______________. I also do not like eggplants and ______________. They are ______________. I also

can't stand ______________. They are rich in protein and vitamins but they are ______________.

<table>
<tr><td colspan="2">

10. Listen and arrange the information in the same order as it occurs in the text

</td></tr>
</table>

	She loves lamb and pork
	She loves spinach and tomatoes
	He also loves French fries
1	**In my family there are four people**
	My sister's favourite food is meat
	My father's favourite food is roast chicken
	We all love food and eat a lot
	I love cakes and sweets.
	My mother's favourite food is vegetables
	I also love honey. It's sweet and healthy.

11. Answer the questions below about Maite

a. How many people are there in Maite's family?

b. What do her parents love?

c. What does her mother hate?

d. What does her brother Rafa love?

e. What does her brother Jaime love?

f. What does Maite love?

g. What does she hate?

h. Why?

12. Listening slalom: follow the speaker from top to bottom and number the boxes accordingly

1	2	3	4
I love (1)	I hate	I can't stand	I love
chocolate	**meat (1)**	spinach	burgers
and cakes	sausages	**because it is (1)**	and tomatoes
or French fries	because they are sweet	because they are	**tasty (1)**
and delicious	disgusting.	**and rich in protein. (1)**	because they are
greasy	**I eat it with salad (1)**	I prefer	even though
they are a bit unhealthy.	and unhealthy.	**or French fries. (1)**	carrots.

1. Listen and fill in the gaps

a. Por lo general desayuno un ________________.

b. A veces desayuno ________________.

c. …pero raramente desayuno ________________.

d. Generalmente almuerzo ________________ con pollo o ________________ con verduras.

e. Por lo general no meriendo ________________.

f. De vez en cuando meriendo pan con ________________.

g. Normalmente ceno ________________.

h. A veces como ________________ o ________________.

2. Mystery VERBS – guess the words, then listen and see how many you guessed right.

a. No __ __ n__ mucho.

b. __ __ __ __ __ y __ __ __ __ pan con mermelada.

c. __ __ b___ mucha agua.

d. __ __ m__ __ __ __ __ carne con ensalada.

e. Me __ __ __ __ __ __ t__ la fruta.

f. __ __ i__ el pescado.

3. Listening for detail: tick which food items Sergio usually eats for breakfast

Lo que desayuno	Huevos
	Fruta
	Queso
	Pan
	Miel
Lo que almuerzo	Pasta
	Carne
	Pollo
	Sopa
	Arroz
Lo que meriendo	Mermelada
	Nocilla (Nutella)
	Pasteles
	Tostada
	Leche
Lo que ceno	Sopa
	Verduras
	Ensalada
	Queso
	Carne
Lo que bebo	Agua
	Café
	Zumo de manzana
	Zumo de naranja
	Café con leche
	Leche

4. Spot the differences and correct your text

Para el desayuno por lo general como poco: un plátano, dos o tres peras, tostadas con miel, un zumo de naranja y una taza de té sin azúcar. El café me gusta dulce.

A mediodía, por lo general, almuerzo solo arroz con pescado o carne y bebo zumo de fruta. Me encanta el pollo picante porque es sano y es rico en vitaminas. A veces como espárragos. Me encantan porque son sabrosos y ricos en vitaminas.

Para la cena no como mucho. Suelo comer arroz y carne con verduras, y de postre tomo un yogur o bebo pasteles.

5. Spot the missing words and write them in

Me llamo Fernando. Por lo general no desayuno. Solo un huevo y de té. El té me gusta dulce, mucho azúcar. A veces bebo zumo. A mediodía almuerzo pollo con verduras y bebo agua. Como muchas verduras porque son sanas y deliciosas. Me gustaría gambas porque me encantan. Después del colegio meriendo dos tostadas y bebo una taza de té. Me encanta la miel deliciosa. Para la como bastante. Suelo comer arroz, mariscos con verduras y uno o dos pasteles.

6. Faulty translation: spot the translation errors and correct them

My name is Roberto. In general, I don't eat much

for lunch. Only an apple and a lot of coffee.

At dinner, I usually eat fish with baked potatoes

and drink mineral water. Sometimes I eat roast

turkey. I often eat burgers because they are tasty.

For dinner, I eat very much, usually rice or a salad.

7. Write in English what each person thinks about each food/drink

	Food	Opinion
1. José		

	Food	Opinion
2. Dylan		

8. Listen, spot and correct the spelling and grammar errors

No desayuno mucha, solo un huevo y una taza de té. Té me gusta muy dulce, con mucha azúcar. A veces bebo piña zumo.

Mediodía, almuerzo asado pollo con verduras y bebo mineral agua. Como muchas verduras porque es muy deliciosa.

Después el colegio, merendo una tostada con mermelada.

Para cena, tomo arroz con pescado o ensalada. A veces como un fresa helado.

9. What do they have at lunch?

	What they eat (three details)
1	
2	
3	
4	
5	
6	
7	

10. Narrow listening - Gapped translation

Usually I don't eat _____________ in the morning: a banana, one or two ____________, bread with

____________, an ____________ juice and cup of coffee _________ __________. It's a very

____________ breakfast rich in vitamins and ____________. At noon I have __________ with

____________ and ____________ . I drink cold lemonade because it __________ and delicious. At dinner

I have a _________ or __________ soup with some ____________. I love icecream because it is

11. Listen and arrange the information in the same order as it occurs in the text

	It is very healthy!
	At noon I eat a lot
	I eat bread with honey or jam
1	**At breakfast I don't eat much**
	I eat meat or chicken with vegetables
	I usually have fish or seafood
	At 4 pm I have my snack
	One or two eggs and a toast
	It is delicious!
	I also drink a coffee without sugar
	I have dinner around 8.30
	I drink 3 litres of water a day

12. Answer the questions below about Enrique

1. What 3 things does he eat at breakfast?

a.

b.

c.

2. How does he describe his breakfast? (two adjectives)

a.

b.

3. What does he usually have for lunch?

a.

b.

c.

d.

4. At what time does he have dinner? ____________

5. What does he have for dinner?

a.

b.

13. Listen to Pablo talk about his family and fill in the grid

	Relationship to speaker	Appetizer	Main course	Dessert
Selina				
Marcela				
Joaquín				
Julián				

UNIT 13 – TALKING ABOUT CLOTHES AND ACCESSORIES

1. Listen and fill in the gaps

a. En casa __________ un chandal.

b. En la playa llevo un ____________.

c. En el gimnasio llevo una __________.

d. Nunca llevo ________.

e. Cuando hace frío llevo una __________.

f. En la discoteca llevo una __________.

g. Mi hermano siempre __________ zapatillas de deporte.

h. Mi novia lleva __________ ____________.

2. Mystery WORDS – guess the words, then listen and see how many you guessed right.

a. Una b__ __ __ __ __ __

b. Una __ __ __ __ s__

c. Una __ __ __d__

d. Un __b__ __ __ __

e. Un __ __ __ __ __ y

f. Un __ __ __j__

g. Un __ __ ñ __ __ __ __

3. Listening for detail: tick the clothes Dylan wears

Lo que llevo cuando hace frío	Una bufanda Un jersey Un abrigo Botas Un bañador
Lo que llevo cuando salgo con mi novia	Una camisa Un cinturón Pantalones Sandalias Zapatos elegantes
Lo que llevo cuando salgo con mis amigos	Una chaqueta deportiva Una falda Un sombrero Un chaleco Zapatillas de deporte
Lo que llevo cuando me quedo en casa	Un jersey Una camiseta Pantuflas Un sombrero Unos vaqueros

4. Spot the differences and correct your text

Me llamo Alejandra. Tengo diecisiete años. Soy bastante deportista y tengo ropa de muchos colores y tipos diferentes.

Prefiero la ropa de mala calidad pero no muy barata. Por lo general, en casa llevo un chándal o una camiseta, pantalones y zapatillas de deporte o botas.

Cuando voy al gimnasio, llevo un abrigo y zapatillas de deporte blancas. Tengo seis chándales diferentes. Son de marca porque las marcas me encantan.

Cuando salgo con mis amigos me pongo una chaqueta negra, vaqueros y zapatillas de deporte.

Cuando salgo con mi hermano me pongo vestidos elegantes y aburridos y mis patos favoritos. También son feos y cómodos.

5. Spot the missing words and write them in

Me llamo Jean-Paul. Tengo dieciocho. Soy Francia. En mi familia cuatro personas y me llevo bien con todos. Tenemos mascotas, un perro, un loro muy hablador y un pez.

Me encanta comprar ropa, sobre todo zapatillas y camisetas de colores diferentes. No tengo ropa, pero me gusta mucho la ropa tengo. Me encanta la ropa. Cuando hace frío, llevo un abrigo y pantalones negros, o morados. A veces llevo una chaqueta. Cuando hace calor, llevo camisas mangas, vaqueros sandalias.

Mis comidas son la pizza, y la pasta. Odio verduras.

6. Faulty translation: correct the translation

I hate clothes. Especially sports clothes. I have many T-shirts. My favourite tracksuit is blue and red. I also have many formal shoes.

At home I usually wear a T-shirt, new jeans and boots.

When I go out with my girlfriend, if it's hot I wear a T-shirt and jeans. If it's cold I wear a long coat and my favourite jeans.

7. Write in English the clothing item/accessory and description

	Noun	Adjective
1		
2		
3		
4		
5		
6		
7		
8		

8. Listen, spot and correct the spelling and grammar errors

Me llamo Sergio. Tengo quince años. Cuando voy a colegio, llevo una camisa azul, pantalón azules y zapatos negro.

En casa por lo general llevo una camiseta, vaqueras y pantufla. Tengo mucho camisetas y vaqueros.

Cuando voy al gimnasio, llevo una camiseta sin mangas, pantalones cortes y zapatillas deporte. Cuando voy al centro commercial con mi amigos llevo una chaqueta, una camisa, unos pantalones negros o gris, y zapatos negros.

9. What are they wearing?

	Four details each
Paola	
Eva	
Silvio	

10. Narrow listening - Gapped translation

Usually, in the winter at home I wear a ______________, ______________ trousers and ______________. In the summer, instead, I wear a ______________, ______________ and ______________. I have a lot of ______________ ______________ but also some ______________ clothes. I like ______________ clothes but they are very expensive so, I don't have ______________. When I go out with my friends or with my ______________ in the ______________, I wear a ______________ T-shirt, ______________, trainers and ______________. However, in the ______________, I wear a coat, Levi's jeans and ______________.

11. Listen and arrange the information in the same order as it occurs in the text

	I live in the south, in the Algarve
	At school I wear a brown shirt
1	**My name is Gabriela**
	I have a big blue parrot
	with jeans and trainers
	At home I wear a tracksuit
	and I live in Portugal
	When I go out I wear a pink T-shirt
	I have three brothers and a sister
	and black trousers

12. Listen to Diego's description of himself and his family and answer the questions below in English

1. Where is he from? (1)

2. How many siblings has he got? (1)

3. What are his favourite foods? (3)

4. Why? (1)

5. What does he usually wear? (3 details)

6. What are his favourite shoes? (2)

7. Who wears jeans and trainers all the time? (1)

8. Who wears elegant clothes? (1)

13. Fill in the grid – What did they buy ?

	Item bought	What for	Colour	Opinion	Price
Vero					
Ana					
Pepe					
Maite					

1. Complete with JUEGO, HAGO or VOY

a. _______________ al ajedrez

b. _______________ pesas

c. _______________ a las cartas

d. _______________ escalada

e. _______________ a la piscina

f. _______________ de marcha

g. _______________ a casa de mi amigo

h. _______________ con mis amigos

2. Complete with the missing syllables

a. Juego al te__ __ __

b. Hago senderis __ __

c. Voy al polideporti__ __

d. Voy de mar__ __ __

e. Hago cicli__ __ __

f. Voy a la monta __ __

g. __ __ __ go al tenis

h. Voy a la pla__ __

i. Voy al par__ __ __

j. Hago nata__ __ __ __

3. Listening for detail: what activities does Amparo do each day? Tick the correct one

Monday	■ Cycling ■ Chess ■ Rock climbing
Tuesday	■ Going to the mountain ■ Swimming ■ Going clubbing
Wednesday	■ Going to the gym ■ Playing basketball ■ Playing tennis
Thursday	■ Jogging ■ Homework ■ Horse riding
Friday	■ Skiing ■ Weights ■ Chess
Saturday	■ Hiking ■ Weights ■ Bike riding
Sunday	■ Swimming ■ Weights ■ Fishing

4. Spot the intruder

Me llamo Tomás Weidner. Soy un alemán. Soy muy deportista. En mi tiempo libre hago mucho deporte. Mi deporte preferido es la escalada libre. Hago escalada casi todos los días. Cuando hace mal tiempo por lo general me quedo en casa y juego al ajedrez o juego a las cartas con mi hermano menor. También me gusta mucho hacer natación. Hago la natación casi todos los fines de semana en la piscina cerca de mi casa.

5. Faulty translation: correct the translation

My name is Laura. I am red-haired and am very friendly and talkative. I am not very sporty. I prefer to read books, to play chess, play cards and go shopping. When the weather is nice I like going hiking and from time to time I go to the park with my boyfriend. I rarely go to the gym. It is very boring in my opinion. I prefer to go jogging.

THE LANGUAGE GYM

<table>
<tr><td colspan="2">

6. What are their favourite hobbies?

</td><td colspan="2">

7. Spot the differences and correct your text

</td></tr>
</table>

6. What are their favourite hobbies?

1. Nina	
2. Sergio	
3. Luana	
4. Juan Pablo	
5. Alejandro	
6. Lola	
7. Mauricio	
8. Javier	
9. Paquita	

7. Spot the differences and correct your text

Me llamo Clive. Soy inglés. Me encanta ir en bici. Lo hacía todos los días con mis amigos. Es mi deporte favorito. A veces hago escalada, footing o senderismo. Son deportes apasionantes. No me gusta el tenis ni el fútbol. Son deportes aburridos. También odio hacer natación. Hago natación muy raramente en la piscina cerca de mi casa. Dos veces a la semana voy de marcha con mi amigo, Julián. Me encanta bailar.

8. Split sentences – Listen and match

1. Hago pesas	a. montaña
2. Juego al	b. tiempo
3. Voy a casa	c. a menudo
4. Voy a la	d. casi nunca
5. Cuando hace buen	e. baloncesto
6. No hago equitación	**f. todos los días**
7. No hago senderismo	g. con mi primo Paco
8. Voy al parque	h. nunca
9. Voy de pesca	i. de mi amigo

9. Listen, spot and correct the grammar/spelling errors

a. Juego ajedrez

b. Voy a casa mi amigo

c. Hago escalada menudo

d. Juego casi nunca al fútbol

e. Voy a polideportivo

f. Voy marcha

g. Cuando hago buen tiempo hago footing

h. Hago bici todos casi los días

10. Mystery words - predict then check

a. __ s __ a __ __d__

b. C __ __ __ __ a__

c. N __ __ __ __ __ __ ó__

d. P __ __ q u __

e. B __ c __

f. __ s __ __í

g. P __ __ c __

h. T __ __ __ __ o

i. L __ __ __ __ __

11. Spot the missing words and write them in

Me llamo Luna, soy italiana. Me encanta ir bici. Voy en bici todos días con mis amigos. Mi deporte favorito.

Hago todos los días. De vez cuando hago escalada, footing, o senderismo. No me gusta el tenis ni fútbol.

También odio natación. Hago muy raramente porque agotador. Dos veces semana voy marcha con mi amigo

Julien. Me encanta bailar en discoteca con mis amigos.

12. Listen to Dylan talk about his friends and fill in the grid below - in English

Name	Age	Description	Favourite food	Favourite clothes	Favourite sport	How often they practise sport
1. Chris						
2. Aaron						
3. Arnoud						
4. Nico						
5. Niels						

13. Narrow listening - Gapped translation

My name is _____________ and I am _____________ years old. I am _____________ and I am a Canarian. I am

not a kind of _____________, I am someone from the beautiful _____________. I live there with my

_____________, two _____________ and one _____________. My parents are very _____________ and

_____________. My brothers are very _____________ and my sister is _____________ _______ helpful. My

favourite foods are _____________ and _____________. I also eat _____________ very often. In my free

time I do a lot of _____________. I play _____________ at school _____________. I often do

_____________ at the gym near my house. Three times a week I _____________ and from time to time I

go to _____________ with my brothers. Besides sport, I also play _____________ and go to

_____________ once a week. I love _____________. Goodbye.

AUTHOR'S NOTE: Please note that the Canary Islands are actually named after the Latin word for dogs "canis" (not because of canaries). Canarians, or Canary Islanders are renowned for being one of the friendliest and most welcoming people in Spain.

1. Listen and 'shadow' the speaker by whispering after them. Then read the text aloud to yourself.

Me llamo José. En mi familia hay 4 personas. A todos nos encanta la comida y comemos mucho. Las verduras son la comida favorita de mi madre. Le encantan las espinacas y los tomates. A mi hermana le encanta la carne. Le encanta el cordero y el cerdo. La comida favorita de mi padre es el pollo asado. También le encantan las patatas fritas. A mí me encantan los pasteles y los caramelos. También me encanta la miel porque es dulce y sana.

2. Listen and 'shadow' the speaker by whispering after them. Then read the text aloud to yourself.

Hola, me llamo Enrique y soy de Jaén. Tengo dos hermanos pero mi favorito se llama Juan Pablo. Mi padre es bombero y mi madre es enfermera. A los dos les gusta su trabajo. Me gusta mi colegio pero es un poco aburrido. Mi clase no me gusta porque es muy pequeña y no tiene ordenador. En mi mochila tengo un estuche, dos libros y dos cuadernos. Sin embargo no tengo ni una goma ni una regla y ¡me hacen falta!

3. Read the text below silently, then underline every 'c' and 'qu' pronounced 'K' like the 'C' in 'cake' and all the 'c' and 'z' pronounced like 'TH' in 'think. Then listen to the audio track check if you got it right

Hola, me llamo Ignacio García y voy a hablar de mis amigos. Mi amigo Chris tiene diecisiete años. Es alto y gracioso. Su comida favorita es pollo con patatas fritas. Siempre lleva un chándal, es su ropa favorita. Su deporte favorito es el fútbol y lo practica cada fin de semana. Mi amigo Aaron tiene dieciséis años. Es bajo y muy perezoso. Su comida favorita es ensalada de tomates con pescado. Siempre lleva una camiseta blanca. Su deporte favorito es el baloncesto y lo hace todos los lunes. Mi amigo Arnoud tiene dieciocho años. Es muy alto y fuerte. Lo que más le gusta comer es patatas fritas con mayonesa. Normalmente lleva zapatos rojos. Son sus favoritos.

4. Listen and 'shadow' the speaker by whispering after them, focusing on the WORDS underlined. Then read the text aloud to yourself.

Hola, soy Iñaki y soy de Cádiz. Tengo dos hermanos, uno menor y otro mayor. Mis comidas favoritas son helados, miel y pasteles. Es porque me encanta la comida dulce. Normalmente llevo una camiseta guay, unos pantalones cortos y unas chanclas. Mis zapatos favoritos son unas zapatillas de deporte negras. Mi hermano mayor lleva vaqueros con chanclas todos los días. Mi prima Vero es abogada, siempre lleva vestidos y trajes elegantes.

5. Listen and 'shadow' the speaker by whispering after them. Then read the text aloud to yourself.

Mi nombre es Julián. ¿Qué me gusta comer? Prefiero la carne, especialmente el cordero. Me encanta porque es sabroso. Me gustan mucho las hamburguesas. También me encantan las salchichas. Las como con patatas fritas. También me gusta mucho la fruta porque es dulce. No me gustan las verduras. Odio los tomates y las zanahorias. Tampoco me gustan las berenjenas y los pepinos. Son horribles. Además, no soporto los huevos. Son ricos en proteínas y vitaminas, pero son asquerosos.

1. Listen and fill in the gaps

a. Cuando tengo _____________ juego al ajedrez

b. Cuando está _______________ hago ciclismo

c. Cuando hace ________________ hago footing

d. Cuando hace _______________ voy a la playa

e. Cuando _____________ voy al centro comercial

f. Entre __________________ no hago deporte

g. Cuando hay _______________ no voy en bici

h. Cuando hay _____________ me quedo en casa

i. Cuando hace _____________ hago los deberes

2. Mystery WORDS – guess the words, then listen and see how many you guessed right.

a. La __ __ __ b__ __

b. El __ __ l __ __

c. El __ __ e __ __ __

d. El __ __ l

e. __ __ __ __ __ j __ __ __

f. Cuando __ __ __ __ v__

g. Está __ __ b__ __ __ __

h. El __ __ __ o

3. Listening for detail: tick the activities these four people do at the weekend

Pablo	Goes jogging Goes to the shopping centre Goes horse riding Does his homework Goes clubbing
Ana	Goes swimming Goes to the shopping centre Goes to the sports centre Plays on the computer Goes to restaurant
Conchi	Goes jogging Goes to the shopping centre Goes horse riding Plays chess Goes to her friend's house

4. Fill in the blanks

¿Qué hago en mi tiempo libre? Muchas cosas. Cuando hace buen tiempo siempre voy al ___________. Me gusta _____________. Entonces hago _____________, solo o con mi _______________. A él también le gusta correr. Además me _______________ hacer escalada y _______________. Por lo tanto, cuando no _______________, hago senderismo en el bosque cerca de mi casa (vivo en el _______________). Cuando está _______________ y hace _______________, me voy a la _______________. Me encanta la _____________ y tomar el _______________. Cuando hace ______ ___________, sobre todo cuando _____________, me quedo en casa. Me meto en_______________, hago los deberes, juego al _______________ con mi hermano mayor o leo una _______________. Me encanta pasar tiempo en _______________.

5. Spot the missing words and write them in

Me llamo Thor. Soy Suecia. Tengo trece. Cuando calor y está despejado voy la piscina y natación. También de pesca con padre en barco. Es poco aburrido pero me gusta todas formas. La noche voy marcha con mis amigos.

Cuando voy a discoteca, por lo general, llevo camiseta y vaqueros. Mi amiga llama Sofía.

Es simpática inteligente. Hace mal tiempo y llueve siempre queda en casa y hace deberes.

6. Faulty translation: correct the translation

In my free time I do lots of sport. First of all, I like singing and playing the guitar. Moreover, I love buying shirts, jackets, shoes and sports clothes. I love to go shopping when it is rainy. When the weather is hot I enjoy going to the beach, hiking in the woods and, when it is nice, I love going to the beach or lake and swimming. When it is foggy I go windsurfing or sailing. In the winter, when it rains, I love to go to the shopping centre with my family. I love surfing.

7. Write in English what each person thinks about different types of weather

	Opinion	Weather	Activity
1	Loves	Hot	Beach
2			
3			
4			
5			
6			
7			
8			

8. Listen, spot and correct the spelling and grammar errors

Me llamo Patricio. Soy di Barcelona pero vivo en Cádiz, en sur de Espana. Soy alto y delgada. Vivo con mi padres y mi hermano major, Jorge. Me llevo muy bien con mis padre. Pasamos muy tiempo junto. Me gusta mucho jugar al ajedrez con mi padre y a la cartas con mi madre. Paso mucho tiempo con mi hermano tambien. Hago deporte juntos, como footing, natación y pesos. En el fin de semana vamos a marcha juntos.

9. Sentence puzzle - listen and rewrite correctly

a. hace me cuando quedo frío en casa

b. hace centro cuando comercial tiempo voy de al mal compras

c. cuando yo mi llueve y padre al jugamos ajedrez

d. mi cuando calor la hace familia a va playa

e. hace damos un en el paseo parque buen tiempo cuando

f. nieva cuando esquí en la hacemos montaña

g. con cuando cielo está hago footing mi el perro despejado

	10. Listen and arrange the information in the same order as it occurs in the text

10. Listen and arrange the information in the same order as it occurs in the text

	It's a boring job.
	I am a student.
	When it's hot I go to the beach.
1	**I live in Cancún, in Mexico.**
	In the summer I work in a shop.
	When it's windy.
	I love sport.
	I am tall and muscular.
	I love to swim.
	I am funny and friendly.
	I also enjoy scuba diving.
	I go sailing.

11. Listen to Denisse and answer the questions below in English

1. Which country is she from? Where is this country located?

2. Where does she live?

3. What is the weather like?

4. What does she do when the weather is bad? (three details)

5. What does she do when the weather is nice? (three details)

12. Listen to Ariela talk about her family and then fill in the grid

	I (Ariela)	My mother	My father	My sister
Personality				
Physique				
Favourite clothes				
What they do in good weather				
What they do in bad weather				
What they do when it is hot				

UNIT 16 – TALKING ABOUT MY DAILY ROUTINE

1. Listen and fill in the gaps

1. Son las seis y __ __ __ __ __ __

2. Es la __ __ __

3. Son las siete y __ __ __ __ __

4. Me levanto a eso de las __ __ __ __

5. Salgo de casa a las __ __ __ __ y media

6. Voy al colegio a las siete __ __ __ __ __ cuarto

7. Almuerzo a __ __ __ __ __ __ __ __

8. Hago mis deberes a __ __ __ de las cinco

9. Me acuesto a eso de __ __ __ nueve

2. Multiple choice quiz: daily routine times

	a	b	c
1	6:00	7:00	9:00
2	10:00	10:05	10:10
3	2:45	3:45	2:15
4	6:15	5:45	6:05
5	11:05	10:55	10:25
6	2:30	2:15	2:20
7	3:15	2:45	2:35
8	12pm	12am	1pm
9	7:20	7:10	7:50
10	8:15	7:45	2:35

3. Which of the following times do you hear in the text? Tick the ones you hear

4:00	7:30
6:00	8:05
6:15	8:25
6:20	12:00
7:20	12:10

4. Write out the times below, then listen to check if they are correct

1. 8:15 = las ocho y cuarto

2. 7:45 =

3. 9:20 =

4. 6:40 =

5. 11:30 =

6. 9:25 =

7. 10:35 =

8. Midnight =

9. Midday =

5. Spot the differences and correct your text

Me llamo Renaud. Soy francés. Siempre me despierto a eso de las seis y media. Luego me ducho y me lavo los dientes enseguida. No desayuno nada por la mañana, pero mi hermano Valerio desayuna cereales en el comedor con mis padres. Voy al colegio en bici a eso de las siete y cuarto. Vuelvo a casa a eso de las cuatro y luego me relajo un poco. Por lo general veo la tele en el salón. Luego navego por internet, veo una serie en Netflix o veo videos de TikTok en mi habitación. Luego, a las ocho, preparo la comida con mi madre en la cocina. Me encanta preparar ensaladas porque son deliciosas. Me acuesto tarde, a eso de las once.

6. Spot the missing words and write them in

Me llamo Fábian. Soy Gibraltar. Tengo un perro en casa. Donde vivo hay muchos. Siempre levanto temprano, a las seis cuarto. Luego voy al gimnasio y deporte. Me ducho vuelvo a casa. Mi hermano Joe muy perezoso e inactivo. Se levanta a las siete. Joe juega al fútbol y nunca hace deporte. Por está muy muy gordo. Por la tarde, tebeos en mi dormitorio o escucho música. semana cuando vuelvo a casa hago deberes en el salón con mi madre. Me gusta porque es muy inteligente y siempre ayuda. Finalmente, me acuesto a las nueve, en dormitorio.

7. Faulty translation: correct the translation

My name is Akiko, I am Chinese. My daily routine is quite simple. In general, I get up early, around 5:00. I go jogging and then I shower and get dressed. Afterwards, around 7:15, I have breakfast with my mother. I usually eat an egg or two and have some cereals. Around 8:00 I leave my house and go to school by bus. I come back home from school at around 3:30. Then, I rest a bit. Generally, I watch a tv series and chat with my friends on social media. From 6:00 to 8:00 I do my homework. I love doing homework! Then, at around 8:15, I have dinner with my family. I don't eat a lot. Only a salad and some meat or fish. Afterwards, I play on my Playstation until 12:00. Finally, I go to bed.

8. Listen and note down in English what Carmen does at each time

Time	Activity
6:30	
7:15	
8:00	
9:15	
3:30	
4:00	
6:30	
10:00	
11.00	

9. Listen, spot and correct the spelling/grammar errors

Me llamo Alex. Soy de Mallorca. Tengo dos perro en casa. Siempre levanto temprano, a las seis cuarto. Luego voy al polideportivo y juego a bádminton. Me ducha cuando vuelvo a casa, pero mi hermano Joe soy muy perezoso y nunca me ducha. Se levanto a las siete. Joe nunca juega fútbol, y nunca hace deporte. Por eso estoy muy muy gordo. Entra semana cuando vuelvo a casa hago mi deberes en el salón con mi madre. Me gusta porque ella es muy inteligente y siempre mi ayuda. Finalmente, me acuesto a la nueve.

10. Listening slalom: follow the speaker and number the boxes accordingly

1. Myriam	2. René	3. Trini	4. Sofía
Me despierto	Me levanto	Me ducho	Salgo del colegio
Luego voy al gimnasio	Luego me levanto	Luego desayuno	Luego me visto
Después vuelvo a casa	Después me visto	Después preparo mi mochila	Después me ducho
Y luego salgo de casa	Y luego salgo de casa	Y luego me peino	Y luego descanso un poco
Finalmente hago mis deberes	Finalmente me visto	Finalmente, mi padre me lleva al colegio en coche	Finalmente voy al colegio

11. Narrow listening - Gapped translation

My name is Pepe. I am ______________. I am from ____________. My daily routine is very ____________. Generally, I get up ____________, at around five thirty. Then I shower and ____________my uniform. ____________, I have breakfast with my brothers. Then I ____________and prepare my ____________. At around ____________past seven I leave home and go to school. I ____________ home at around four. Then I rest ____________. Generally I read my ____________comics. From six to ____________I do my homework. Then, at eight, I have ____________. I don't eat ____________. Afterwards, I read a ____________or go on the ____________. Then I ____________at 10:35.

12. Fill in the grid: What do the different people do?

	I	My mother	My father	My sister
At 7:30				
At 8:15				
At 12:00				
From 3:00 to 4:00				
From 6:00 to 8:00				
From 8:30 to 11:00				

1. Multiple choice quiz

	a	b	c
1. Yo vivo	en una casa	en un piso	en una granja
2. Mis abuelos viven	en el centro	en las afueras	en la montaña
3. Mis tíos viven	en el campo	en una zona residencial	en el centro
4. Mi mejor amigo vive	en la costa	cerca de la playa	en el centro
5. Mis abuelos maternos viven	a orillas del mar	en el campo	en la montaña
6. Mis abuelos paternos viven	en una casa nueva	en una casa vieja	en una casa fea

2. Listening slalom: follow the speaker from top to bottom and number the boxes accordingly

1	2	3	4
Vivo en una casa (1)	Vivo en un piso	Vivo en un chalet	En mi casa
viejo	**grande y bonita (1)**	hay seis	pequeño
pero bastante acogedor	habitaciones.	**en las afueras (1)**	pero muy acogedor
Mi habitación	en la costa.	en la montaña.	**de Madrid. (1)**
Mi habitación	preferida	**Me encanta mi casa (1)**	Mi cuarto
favorito es	**porque es (1)**	preferida es	es
la terraza.	el salón.	**nueva y moderna. (1)**	mi dormitorio.

3. Spot the differences and correct your text

Me llamo Miquel y era de Vic, cerca de Barcelona. Tengo quince años. Tengo el pelo castaño y los ojos azules. Físicamente soy alto y gordo. De carácter soy tímido y bastante gracioso. Me llevo bien con mi familia porque son todos muy generosos. Mi comida preferida es el marisco. La como todos los días, como el caracol. Soy muy deportista, y en mi tiempo libre me gusta hacer puenting, jugar al tenis, ir al cine y hacer equitación. Por lo general, me acuesto muy temprano, a eso de las seis y me acuesto a mediodía. Vivo en una casa muy vieja y grande en el centro de Barcelona, en las Ramblas. Me encanta mi casa. Mi habitación favorita es el salón porque es muy grande y está muy bien amueblado.

4. Spot the missing words and write them in

Me llamo Fabrizio. Soy Italia. Vivo en casa grande y bonita en la costa. Me gusta. En mi casa diez habitaciones y mi habitación favorita la cocina. Me gusta cocinar en la con mi madre. Siempre me levanto, me ducho en el cuarto y luego me visto en mi dormitorio. Juego el ordenador menudo en el salón. Mi amigo Pablo vive en una casa en la montaña. Es una casa muy vieja muy acogedora. Pablo es gracioso y trabajador. No gusta su casa porque es muy pequeña.

5. Faulty translation: correct the translation

My name is Ramón, I am from Barcelona, in Madrid. My house is in the centre of the city and I live far from the coast. In my house I speak Catalan and Spanish. Catalan is a beautiful and very new language. I live in a big, clean and beautiful apartment. The rooms are very tiny. I have a huge garden with a small table. My horse lives in the garden. Its name is Paco. My favourite thing in my apartment is the kitchen because I love eating. I love relaxing in my living room. I always watch movies and series on Netflix. I also do my sport in there.

6. Fill in the grid

	Description of house	Favourite part of the house
1		
2		
3		
4		
5		
6		
7		
8		

7. Gapped sentences

a. Vivo en una casa grande y __________________.

b. Mi casa está en las ______________ de Valencia.

c. También tengo una casa en el ________________.

d. Mi mejor amigo vive en un piso muy

______________ en el centro de la ________________.

e. Mi novia vive en una zona ______________ en la

______________ en un piso muy ______________.

f. Mis abuelos viven en la __________________.

g. Mi tío favorito, Alfonso, vive en un ______________

de pisos en el centro de Madrid.

8. Listen, spot and correct the spelling and grammar errors

Me llamo Penny. Soy ingles y vivo en un casa muy viejo pero muy bonita en el campo, a Italia. ¡Me encanto mi casa! En mi casa tiene 5 habitacion pero mi habitación favorito es el salón. Todos las días, después de colegio me gusta relajarse en el salón y ver el televisión con mi hermana. ¡No me gusta el cuarto di baño porque a veces hay rata! Tenemos una juegos sala bastante grande donde mi hermano y yo juegamos a la Play.

9. Complete (in English) with the correct details

	Consuelo	Felipe	Jaime
Town			
Description of house (2 details)			
Location of house			
Favourite room			
Another room they like			
Room they hate			

10. Narrow listening - Gapped translation

My house is very ___________ and cosy. It is situated on the ___________ of Cádiz, a city in the south of Spain, on the ___________, ___________ minutes away from La Caleta ___________. I live in a ___________ ___________. In my house there are six rooms: a kitchen, a bathroom, a living room, and three ___________. My favourite room is the ___________ because it is ___________, well-furnished and beautiful. I also like my ___________ because I have my Playstation and my ___________. I like to ___________ and do my homework in there. I hate the ___________ because it is too ___________ and old. It also smells very ___________.

11. Answer the questions in English

1. How old is Oscar?

2. Where is he from?

3. Where does he live?

4. What does he look like? (3 details)

5. What is his character like? (3 details)

6. What are his favourite clothes? (2 details)

7. What's his favourite food? (2 details)

8. At what time does he wake up?

9. After school he goes for a walk with ___________________ and then he ___________________.

10. Does he live in a house or in a flat?

11. What is his house/flat like? (2 details)

12. What is his favourite room?

13. What is the room he hates the most?

14. What does he say about his bedroom? (2 details)

1. Mosaic listening - follow the speaker from <u>left</u> to <u>right</u> → and number accordingly

1	**A eso de las siete (1)**	preparo la comida	y juego con el ordenador	en mi dormitorio
2	Por lo general	**desayuno (1)**	películas	en la sala de juegos
3	Cuando tengo tiempo	escucho música y	**en la cocina (1)**	en el salón
4	A menudo	ayudo	con mi madre	**con mis hermanos (1)**
5	A veces	me meto en Internet	hago los deberes	en el jardín
6	Todos los fines de semana	veo	a mi padre	en la cocina

2. Listen and fill in the gaps

a. A menudo ________________ con mi madre en la cocina.

b. De vez en cuando juego a la Play en la sala de ______________.

c. Dos veces a la semana ______________ en bici.

d. A menudo preparo la comida en la ______________.

e. Siempre hago mis deberes en el ______________.

f. Por lo general me ducho en el ______________ de baño de mis padres.

g. Cuando hace buen tiempo, ______________ revistas en el jardín.

h. Nunca ______________ la tele en ___ salón con mis padres.

3. Break the flow

a. Nuncaveolateleconmispadresenelsalón

b. Porlogeneralpongomibicienelgaraje

c. TodoslosdíassubofotosaInstagram

d. Unaodosvecesalasemanapreparolacomidaenlacocina

e. Nuncadesayunoconmishermanosenelcomedor

f. Porlogeneraldespuésdelcolegioveolateleenmidormitorio

4. Faulty translation: what, how often, where? Listen and correct the errors

	What do they do	How often	Where
1	Chats with his mother	sometimes	on the terrace
2	Helps father	once a week	in the garage
3	Watches TV	every day	in the living room
4	Does homework	five times a week	in the living-room
5	Goes on the Internet	often	in his parents' room
6	Has breakfast	every day	in the dining room
7	Prepares food	never	in the kitchen
8	Rides his bike	from time to time	in the living room

5. Likely or Unlikely? – write L or U next for each sentence you hear explaining why

1		
2		
3		
4		
5		
6		
7		
8		

6. List the activities in the correct order in which Felipe does them (there is a small amount of extra information for each sentence in the recording)

	I do my homework
	I go on the internet
	I listen to music
1	**I have breakfast**
	I read my favourite comics
	I leave the house
	I watch a movie
	I brush my teeth
	I rest in my bed

7. Listen to the verbs and add them in where appropriate (they are not in the right order!)

a. ______________ con mi madre

b. ______________ en bici

c. ______________ la comida

d. ______________ mis deberes

e. ______________ los dientes

f. ______________ cereales

g. ______________ fotos a Instagram

d. ______________ películas

8. Narrow listening - Gapped translation

___________ ___________I get up at five in the morning. Then I _________and have breakfast in the _________.

After that I brush my teeth and _________my _________. Then, I _______________ and go to school at

_________. Generally, I go by _________. When I _________ _________, I chat on Skype with my family in

Australia and go on the internet in my _________. Then, I _______________in the garden with my two

_________. Sometimes I watch _________ and upload photos to Instagram in my _________ _________.

Usually, I have dinner at around _________. After dinner I _________ _________ and then shower. After that

I read my favourite _________ and go to bed at _________.

9. Sentence puzzle – Listen and rewrite correctly

1. despierto temprano, Siempre me de las seis a eso menos diez

2. Para solo como el desayuno hervido y dos tostadas un huevo con mermelada

3. Salgo de menos cuarto casa a las siete y en bici voy al colegio

4. Tengo y antipático que se llama un hermano muy perezoso Joe y es

5. días monto Todos los en bici en con mis el jardín dos perros

6. Por o sola lo general, cenar veo después de el salón con la tele en mis padres,

10. Answer the questions about Maya
(EXTENSION: Write down some extra details that you hear)

1. At what time does she usually get up?

2. How does she go to school?

3. What is her favourite school subject?

4. What two sports does she usually do after school?

5. Where does she usually chat with her mother?

6. In which room does she do her homework?

7. What does she never do during dinner?

8. What three things does she always do after dinner?

9. What two things does she do before going to bed?

10. At what time does she go to bed?

READING ALOUD – Part 3

1.Read the text below silently, focusing especially on the words in bold. Then listen to the audio track to check if you got the pronunciation right and have a go at reading it aloud.

Hola, yo me llamo <u>Ariela</u>. Soy <u>graciosa</u> y también alta. Mi ropa favorita son mis <u>vaqueros viejos</u>. Son <u>viejos</u> pero cómodos. Cuando <u>hace</u> buen tiempo <u>hago</u> footing y <u>voy</u> al parque. Cuando <u>hace</u> mal tiempo juego al <u>ajedrez</u> y veo la tele. Cuando <u>hace</u> calor siempre <u>voy</u> a la playa.

Mi madre es amable y <u>alegre</u>. Siempre <u>lleva</u> un vestido blanco. Es su <u>favorito</u>. Cuando <u>hace</u> buen tiempo mi madre va de <u>paseo</u> con el perro. También <u>juega</u> al tenis. Cuando <u>hace</u> mal tiempo <u>ve</u> series en la tele y <u>juega</u> a las cartas con su <u>mejor</u> amigo.

Mi padre es <u>trabajador</u> y muy guapo. Prefiere <u>llevar</u> una camisa negra. Cuando <u>hace</u> buen tiempo <u>hace</u> <u>equitación</u> y va a la <u>piscina</u>; pero cuando <u>hace</u> mal tiempo <u>juega</u> a las cartas o <u>hace su trabajo</u>. No le gusta el calor, <u>así que</u> cuando <u>hace</u> calor se <u>queda</u> en casa.

Mi <u>hermana</u> es <u>perezosa</u> y delgada. Siempre <u>lleva</u> una camiseta rosa. Es su favorita. Cuando <u>hace</u> buen tiempo siempre <u>va</u> a la playa y toma el sol. Sin embargo, cuando <u>hace</u> mal tiempo prefiere <u>leer</u> libros y escuchar música. Cuando <u>hace</u> calor ella siempre va al parque.

---

2. Underline any word you are not sure you can pronounce correctly. Then listen to the audio track focusing on those words and read the text aloud to yourself.

Me llamo Carlos, soy español. Mi rutina diaria es muy simple. En general, me levanto muy temprano, a eso de las 5:00. Hago footing y luego me ducho y desayuno. Después, a eso de las 6:45, desayuno con mi madre. Normalmente como un huevo o dos y tomo un poco de pan. A eso de las 8:00 salgo de la casa y voy al colegio en bicicleta. Vuelvo a casa a eso de las 4:30. Entonces, descanso un poco. En general, veo una película y chateo con mis amigos en Whatsapp. De 6:00 a 8:00 hago mis deberes. ¡Odio hacer mis deberes! Luego, a eso de las 7:45, ceno con mi familia. No como mucho. Solo una ensalada y algo de pollo o pescado. Después, juego a la Play hasta las 11:00. Finalmente, me acuesto.

3. Underline any word you are not sure you can pronounce correctly. Then listen to the audio track focusing on those words and read the text aloud to yourself.

1. Hola, ¡soy Marco! Soy de Bilbao y vivo en una casa vieja y pequeña en las afueras de la ciudad. ¿Mi habitación favorita? Pues, la cocina, pero también me gusta mi dormitorio. Sin embargo, nuestro comedor es feísimo. Lo odio.

2. Hola, soy Felipe y soy de Ceuta. Mi casa es muy bonita y espaciosa. Vivo en el centro de la ciudad. Mi habitación favorita tiene que ser mi dormitorio, aunque el jardín también está bien. La habitación que odio es el salón. Es frío y oscuro.

3. Hola, soy Jaime y soy de Melilla. Mi casa es nueva, pero fea. Vivo en el campo. Mi habitación favorita es el salón, y también me gusta la sala de juegos. Sin embargo, nuestro cuarto de baño es horrible. ¡Siempre hay cucarachas enormes!

UNIT 19 – TALKING ABOUT FUTURE PLANS AND HOLIDAYS

1. Listen and fill in the gaps

1. Este verano __________ a ir de vacaciones a Cuba.

2. Voy a viajar en ______________.

3. Vamos a ___________ una semana allí.

4. ____________ divertido.

5. Voy a ______________ en un hotel de lujo.

6. Voy a ______________.

7. Vamos a ____ ____ ____________.

8. Me gustaría ____________ ____________.

9. Nos gustaría ____________ ____________.

2. Spot the differences and correct your text

a. Este invierno voy a ir de vacaciones a México.

b. Voy a pasar tres días allí.

c. Voy a ir con mi novio.

d. Vamos a quedarnos en un hotel caro.

e. Voy a hacer mis deberes.

f. Mi hermana va a comprar regalos.

g. Vamos a ir a la piscina.

h. Voy a beber Zumosol.

i. Me gustaría ir al museo.

j. Nos gustaría ir de pesca.

3. Listen and tick the correct details

Pablo	va a ir a Japón va a ir en barco va a quedarse en un hotel de lujo va a comer mucho Sushi va a ir de marcha
Ana	va a ir a Italia va a ir en tren va a quedarse en un camping va a hacer turismo va a comer mucha pasta y pizza
Conchi	va a ir a Francia va a ir en bici va a quedarse en un albergue juvenil va a ir a la playa va a visitar sitios históricos
Selina	va a ir a Grecia va a ir en avión y en barco va a hacer buceo va a hacer turismo va a comer mucha ensalada griega

4. Write in the missing words

Este verano voy a ir ________ vacaciones a Roma, ________ Italia. Voy ________ ir en avión. Vamos a pasar una semana ________. Vamos ________ quedarnos en un hotel ________ lujo. ________ voy a ir de marcha. Mis hermanas van a ir ____________ compras y mis padres van ____________ comprar recuerdos y a hacer turismo porque ________ muchos sitios históricos ____________.

5. Guess what comes next then listen to see how many you guessed right

a. Voy a ir de vacaciones en ____________.

b. Voy a pasar ____________ dias allí.

c. Voy a quedarme en ____ ____________.

d. Por la mañana voy a ir ____ ____ ________.

e. Por la tarde voy a hacer ____________.

f. Por la noche voy a ir ____ ____________.

6. Multiple choice quiz

	a	b	c
1	He is Swiss	He is Swedish	He is Russian
2	He is travelling by train	He is travelling by plane	He is travelling by boat
3	He is travelling alone	He is travelling with his friend	He is travelling with his family
4	He is staying in a cheap hotel	He is staying in a three-star hotel	He is staying in a luxury hotel
5	He is staying there for two weeks	He is staying there for three weeks	He is staying there for ten days
6	He is going to scuba dive	He is going to go clubbing	He is going to eat and sleep
7	He will also go sightseeing	He will also go shopping	He will also sunbathe
8	It will be fun	It will be cool	It will be expensive

7. Faulty translation: spot the translation errors and correct them

This winter I am going on holiday to Cuba. I am going there by train. I am going to go there with my brother. We are going to spend ten seconds there. We are going to stay in a lovely hotel in La Habana, the capital of Cuba. It is a loud place with a great nightlife. There are lots of museums and our hotel is very far from the beach. Every day I am going to go to the mountains. In the morning I am going to swim and surf. I will also go fishing. In the afternoon we will sleep. My parents will read books and my sister will buy lots of clothes, as always. For dinner we will go to Spanish restaurants. We will eat a lot of meat and pasta. We will also listen to a lot of Salsa, the famous Cuban dance.

8. Listen, spot and correct the spelling and grammar errors

Esto verano voy ir de vacaciones avión. Voy pasar dos semana allí. Voy a ir con mi toda familia. Vamos a quedarme en un hotel de luxo con piscina cerca de la playa. Por manana vamos a ir a la playa. Por la tarde vamos a ir compras y a hacer turismo. A eso de las ocho vamos cenar en restaurants locales para comer platos típico. Por la noche, mi hermana y yo voy a ir de marcha. También, me gustarían aprender a bailar salsa. Lo pasaramos bomba.

9. Complete with the correct details (English)

Holiday destination	
Means of transport	
Duration	
Who with	
Accommodation	
Activities	

10. Listen and arrange the information in the same order as it occurs in the text

1	My name is Gabriela
	We are going to stay there nine days
	This summer I am going to go on Holiday to Costa Rica
	The hotel is near the beach
	We are going to sunbathe
	We are going to go by ship
	We are going to go to the beach every day
	We are going to stay in a four-star hotel
	We are going back home on 13 July
	We are going to scuba dive
	I am going to go with my best friends
	At night we are going to go clubbing

11. Listen to Carlos and answer the questions below in English

1. Where is he going on holiday? (two details)

2. When does his holiday begin?

3. How long for?

4. How is he travelling?

5. Who with?

6. Who are they staying with?

7. What is the name of the town where they will stay?

8. What are they going to do there? (4 details)

a.

b.

c.

d.

12. Fill in the grid in English

	Carolina	Benicio	Sofía	Mateo
Destination				
Who with				
Departure date				
How long for				
Accommodation				
Location				
Activities				